what Jane Austen taught me about love & romance

DEBRA WHITE SMITH

HARVEST HOUSE PUBLISHERS

EUGENE, OREGON

Cover by Koechel Peterson & Associates, Inc., Minneapolis, Minnesota

Debra White Smith: Published in association with the literary agency of Alive Communications, Inc., 7680 Goddard Street, Ste #200, Colorado Springs, CO 80920. www.alivecommunications.com.

WHAT JANE AUSTEN TAUGHT ME ABOUT LOVE AND ROMANCE
Copyright © 2007 by Debra White Smith
Published by Harvest House Publishers
Eugene, Oregon 97402
www.harvesthousepublishers.com

Library of Congress Cataloging-in-Publication Data
Smith, Debra White.
    What Jane Austen taught me about love and romance / Debra White Smith.
        p. cm.
        ISBN-13: 978-0-7369-1889-3
        ISBN-10: 0-7369-1889-2
        1. Bible. N.T. Corinthians, 1st, XIII, 1-8—Criticism, interpretation, etc. 2. Love—
        Biblical teaching. 3. Austen, Jane, 1775–1817—Criticism and interpretation. I. Title.
    BS2675.52.S65 2007
    823'.7—dc22

                                                                    2006022944

Printed in the United States of America

        07 08 09 10 11 12 13 14 15 / VP-SK / 10 9 8 7 6 5 4 3 2 1

To my sisters-in-love, the
Amen Sister Girlfriend Holy Water Revival
Chicks: Kevon, Dim, and Donna.
I love you!

Acknowledgments

Special thanks to Terry Glaspey for coming up with the idea for this book in the first place and for all the great feedback. Terry is the unsung hero of this project.

Contents

Love is patient, love is kind.
It does not envy, it does not boast, it is not proud.
It is not rude, it is not self-seeking, it is not easily angered,
it keeps no record of wrongs.
Love does not delight in evil but rejoices with the truth.
It always protects, always trusts,
always hopes, always perseveres.
Love never fails.

~ 1 CORINTHIANS 13:4-8 ~

Love is patient…

Emma Woodhouse and Sir Patience Extraordinaire

Adopt the pace of nature: her secret is patience.
~ RALPH WALDO EMERSON ~

I'll never forget the first time I fully encountered Jane Austen. I was in a college class as an undergraduate and the professor assigned *Pride and Prejudice*. I'd read about Jane Austen in previous literature classes but had yet to fully embrace her. Once I read through *P & P*, my first reaction was less than impressive. To put it bluntly, it was downright stupid.

I remember spouting something like, "I'd like to tell these characters to get a life, get a job, get a hobby. All they do is sit around and talk about who's going to get married." Looking back, I now realize what my professor must have realized: I'd barely scratched the surface of Austen.

But Jane patiently waited for my literary side to mature. I

continued to circle her works and come to terms with what she was all about. By the time I landed in graduate school, I'd rolled around in Jane enough that my views had changed. I'd fallen in love with Austen's wittiness, her characters, and the dynamics of the plots. (Watching the Arts and Entertainment movies didn't hurt either. They brought her characters and plots to life in a way that enhanced the text.) I gradually became so impressed with Austen that I decided to do my master's thesis on her.

And that's when my vision for presenting all her novels with contemporary storylines took root. Several years later my vision became a reality, and I published *The Austen Series* (Harvest House Publishers). That experience revolutionized my abilities to create characters.

One of my top-five favorite characters to recreate was Emma Woodhouse. I named her Amanda, plopped her into twenty-first century Tasmania, Australia, and tried to produce as much spark and friction between her and "Nate Knighton" as Austen displays between Emma and George Knightley.

My favorite part from *Emma* is the closing scene when George Knightley tells Emma he loves her:

> "My dearest Emma," said [Knightley], "for dearest you will always be, whatever the event of this hour's conversation, my dearest, most beloved Emma—tell me at once. Say 'No,' if it is to be said." She could really say nothing. "You are silent," he cried, with great animation; "absolutely silent! At present I ask no more."

Emma was almost ready to sink under the agitation of this moment. The dread of being awakened from the happiest dream was perhaps the most prominent feeling.

…Seldom, very seldom does complete truth belong to any human disclosure…Mr. Knightley could not impute to Emma a more relenting heart than she possessed, or a heart more disposed to accept of his…She was his own Emma, by hand and word, when they returned into the house.[1]

You can feel how Knightley longs for Emma and dares to hope that she might return his love. I adore the movie rendition of this scene. I remember watching it and aching for Emma and Knightley until I thought I was going to burst. All through *Emma*, Knightley eats his heart out over her. But for the longest time, Emma is blissfully ignorant of his love and views him as a brother.

I'm reminded of that old Frankie Valli song "My Eyes Adored You," which details the story of a man who adored a girl in childhood. He was in sixth grade. She was in fifth grade. They went back a long way. But he never laid a hand on her, simply admired her while he carried her books from school. Eventually, the boy grew into a man, became famous, made a name for himself, but he always remembers that girl he left behind and the life with her he'll never have.

Fortunately Austen's *Emma* doesn't end that way. George Knightley wins his woman, and Emma embraces her Knightley. First Corinthians 13:4 states, "Love is patient," and Knightley's patience is well worth his prize. He is "Sir Patience Extraordinaire."

When I wrote *Amanda*, I put Nate Knighton through as much anguish as Austen puts Knightley through. The poor guy is nearly sweating blood by the time he admits his love to Amanda and realizes Amanda loves him—and only him. Just as Knightley is Emma's brother figure, so Nate is Amanda's. And the woman who's bent on being the queen of matchmakers can barely see past the brotherly image to the hunk-of-a-guy who adores her. Finally, about the time Nate's patience is wearing thin, Amanda wakes up and lays a kiss on him he won't forget.

According to Jean Jacques Rousseau, "Patience is bitter, but its fruit is sweet." The problem is, most people are like my Knighton and Austen's Knightley and don't enjoy waiting for that fruit. That's where the bitterness comes in. With any situation where patience is required, a wait is usually a major element of the picture. Most waiting periods fall into a pattern or *Stages of Patience* that Jane Austen reveals in George Knightley and other characters whom she puts through the "Austen Torture Chamber of Patience." Through her intricately woven plots, Jane brilliantly depicts five stages that bring her characters to life because they are also manifested in real people as they struggle with real life. These stages are 1) Recognition of the problem, 2) Frustration, 3) Confrontation, 4) Withdrawal, and 5) Resolution.

Ponder your own life for a minute and the problems you've faced that required patience. As you read the following observations from *Emma*, ask yourself if you've allowed God to bring you through the *Stages of Patience* to complete what He wants you to learn.

> *He that can have patience can have what he will.*
> BENJAMIN FRANKLIN

Stage 1: Recognition of the Problem

I remember being in junior high and liking a guy who seemed to notice every girl *but* me. I felt as invisible as Knightley feels. I recall the futile longing mixed with frustration so poignantly it's almost as if the situation occurred yesterday. Looking back, I'm glad Conner never woke up like Emma did. I was far too young for the going-steady romance that I dreamed of, and Conner was way too immature.

Meanwhile, there was another young man, Rob, who was as enamored with me as I was with Conner. But as these things go, I wasn't remotely interested in Rob. I have no doubt that he pined after me as much as I pined after my elusive man.

I'm sure Knightley would agree that love triangles are only intriguing when you *aren't* part of one. Unlike Knightley, nobody's patience paid off in my situation. I never got my man, and the other guy never got me. What frustration for ones so young!

In order to realize they need patience, people first have to recognize that there is a problem that tempts them to respond *impatiently*. Numerous Austen characters find themselves in such situations. However, George Knightley plays the star role for a character being dumped into a serious problem: He has fallen in love with a woman who is as romantic about him as Conner was about me.

When Knightley first mentions Emma and matrimony, he wants her to be *in* love but also in doubt that the man will love her back. Even though he thinks Emma's character could be improved by such an experience, he only wishes her in love in a "safe" circumstance—the man not being equally enamored with her. In the same conversation, Knightley also says he loves to look at Emma and has never met a woman he thinks is better looking. Although he is already clearly attracted to Emma, he has yet to recognize the extent.

Only when Frank Churchill comes on the scene does Knightley get a clue that he has a problem. The "clue" hits him hard when Emma begins to do what she's vowed she won't do—make eyes at a man with thoughts of matrimony. That man is Churchill. At this point, Knightley recognizes that he's in a fix. As a result, he slams Frank and calls him a "trifling fellow," which translates into modern language as "shallow idiot." Actually, Frank Churchill really isn't that bad of a guy. But Knightley, who loves to look at Emma, is jealous and frustrated because Emma is looking at someone else.

Stage 2: Frustration

Frustration knew no end for me when the guy I was "in love" with in junior high had the audacity to go steady with another girl. Of all the nerve! I remember being as jealous of her as Knightley is of Churchill. Even today, I don't know what in the world Conner saw in her. She was as skinny as a toothpick and wasn't the least bit pretty—not in my opinion anyway. I mean, whoever thought blonde hair and blue eyes and a glossy-lipped grin was pretty anyway? Conner must have been blind.

But Knightley isn't. He sees Emma exactly for what she is—a fascinating female who is witty, charming, and a little too sassy and confident for her own good. Austen brilliantly sketches Knightley's frustration as he sinks more deeply in love with Emma, and she remains focused upon Frank Churchill.

Knightley's agony peeks when Emma is planning to attend a ball that will involve Churchill. Knightley provokes Emma and says he'd rather be looking over accounts than going to a dance. Later, when the dance is canceled, Knightley mocks Emma. He is, of course, beyond relieved that Emma won't be dancing with Frank. While George Knightley's frustration grows, so grows his verbal barbs against Churchill, moving from negative innuendoes to blatant insults.

Frustration is that awful, uptight feeling we get when we believe we are powerless to stop the situation that holds us captive and requires our patience. The longer the situation stretches, the more uptight we can become. In the face of such, a person's frustration can mount to the point that he (or she) might find it difficult to hold his tongue. Squelching opinions of the situation or people can become impossible. From this stance, we often build to the point of some form of confrontation.

Thankfully, I never attempted to confront the female who snared Conner. I was too young and, really, had no right. However, Knightley is grown up and he does confront Emma.

Stage 3: Confrontation

I recall one Christmas break when Conner miraculously woke up and realized I was alive. Honestly, I can't remember if this happened before or after the blonde-haired distraction. However, I do remember the guy coming to see me. I was very excited, to say the least—so excited I became horribly nauseous. And I'd had spaghetti for breakfast. Not the best choice for the occasion.

So there I was, a lovesick 14-year-old with spaghetti on a churning stomach. My parents agreed to let me out of their sight for a broad-daylight drive to the country store, which you could almost see from our house. Everything was fine on the way to the store except for the fact that my nausea was growing to mammoth proportions. By the time we got out, got our Cokes, and got back into the truck, my nausea was threatening its boundaries.

But my desire to "be cool" was much stronger than the fraction of common sense I possessed. Instead of asking Conner to pull over, I kept resisting the bulge pushing against my throat. Finally, without any warning, I threw up all over the inside of the guy's truck. Well, it was his dad's truck. I'm sure his father was just *thrilled* when Conner got home that day.

When I got home and told my parents and sister I'd regurgitated all over Conner's truck, they showed me a good deal of sympathy. After nearly 30 years, I just now found out they all laughed at me behind my back. Of all the nerve!

All that is to say that while I never confronted my dream hunk about his other girl, he did have an up-close and graphic "confrontation" with the contents of my stomach. After that, he pretty much withdrew from my life. Vomiting isn't exactly the stuff dream dates are made of.

Jane Austen sketches George Knightley as one who is mature. He does a remarkable job of handling the confrontation with Emma over Frank Churchill. By the time Knightley mentions the issues to Emma, he has measured the situation and decided a frank conversation is a must. However, unknown to Knightley, by the time he has the talk with Emma, she has already decided she is not in love with Frank and that Harriet should be. But all Knightley can see is Frank's flirting with Emma while the subtle clues point to his being attached to Jane Fairfax.

Finally Knightley resolves to tell Emma he believes Frank and Jane are attached because it is his duty as a "friend" to do so. Much to Knightley's dismay, Emma denies that Frank could be attached to Jane at all. Knightley is so dismayed, he leaves. Even though Knightley is stunned and fully believes Emma is deceived, he doesn't erupt or go into an impatient frenzy. He just quietly withdraws from the scene. Later, after chastising Emma for her rudeness to Miss Bates, he leaves the area altogether to go visit his brother. He completely distances himself from Emma.

Stage 4: Withdrawal

I've never thrown up on another guy in my life. However, I believe if I'd thrown up on my husband when we were dating, he'd have felt genuinely sorry for me and *not* laughed at me. Why? Because he truly cares for me. Conner told his friends what happened, and they all had a good laugh. I still figure his dad *never* laughed.

There's not much more humiliating to a 14-year-old girl than throwing up on the school hunk. After I found out Conner told his friends, I withdrew from him too. But I still pined after his handsome self. Unlike Emma and Knightley, my withdrawal stage didn't produce a fulfilled romance. The guy never even called to see if I were dead or alive, so I learned he didn't really care about me after all. The other important lesson I learned during the withdrawal stage was never to eat spaghetti for breakfast.

Sometimes the hardest thing to do is to take our hands off a stressful situation and allow God to do His work. Often in the face of completing everything possible to the best of our abilities, withdrawal is the best recourse. Sometimes that means emotional withdrawal; other times it involves physical withdrawal, even taking a full break from or ending a relationship.

Knightley chooses to vamoose. In his distress, he goes to visit his brother and sister-in-law. Hitting the trail often goes a long way toward improving a bad situation—or at least the way you feel about it. Emma herself thinks the equivalent of "absence makes the heart grow fonder." But little does Emma or Knightley know that his absence will catapult her from fondness to true love.

After he leaves, Emma learns that her friend Harriet has decided *she* is in love with Knightley. Emma gets a cold bucket of water in the face. She's shocked into thinking "that Mr. Knightley must marry no one but herself!"[2] Unknown to Emma, this is exactly what Knightley dreams of. From here, Emma comes to the conclusion Knightley has tried to communicate to her: that she shouldn't have tried to arrange everyone's love life for them. And all this occurs, not because of a convincing speech from Knightley, but during his absence.

Often, at the height of our impatience, we say and do things that aren't as powerful as our absence or our silence would be. When Knightley confronts Emma with the truth of Frank Churchill's attachment to Jane Fairfax, it is only in his absence and silence that Emma learns he was right about Frank...and so much more.

In our own lives, so many times we underestimate the hand of God to work in our silence. Once we bravely step forward and lovingly confront, the temptation to repeat a confrontation can seem too strong to ignore, especially if we are so impatient we're pulling out our hair. However, simply stating the truth and then quietly withdrawing usually work together to create a powerful change in situation and thought, which many times lead to a satisfying resolution. In real life the resolution might mean accepting that an exasperating person will never change and that it's perfectly fine to keep a healthy distance in order to maintain our sanity; or, if our sanity is no longer a possibility, at *least* to maintain a peaceful life. With Knightley, the resolution involves the fulfillment of his dreams. He gets his woman!

Stage 5: Resolution

After hearing the news of Frank and Jane's engagement,

Knightley approaches Emma to discover how she is enduring the shock. He still believes Emma is in love with Frank, but soon discovers he's wrong. One thing leads to another until Knightley begins his famous speech: "My dearest Emma, for dearest you will always be...my dearest, most beloved Emma."[3] With these words Knightley ushers in the satisfying resolution to his dilemma. He tells Emma he loves her. *Sigh.* She admits what she has learned in his absence: that she too loves him. And Knightley's patience pays off.

There are many situations and circumstances in life that demand our patience. Some people might readily identify with George Knightley while he waits for his one true love and fears the outcome will be anything but happily ever after. Others might wait to have children and fear they'll never become parents. Or perhaps the child that showed so much potential grows up to become a prodigal, leaving parents to despair if the child will ever succeed. Then there are career promotions that are long in coming, delayed raises, and other employees who receive accolades while our personal efforts are ignored.

Ecclesiastes 3:1 states, "There is a time for everything, and a season for every activity under heaven." Often the key to having more patience involves recognizing what stage of patience we are in and following God's timing for when to make the moves that will resolve the situation. Sometimes that might mean accepting the situation and adapting our expectations and choices to overcome the problem. For my junior high self, this involved accepting that Conner didn't care for me. Other adaptations might include adopting a child who needs a home rather than continuing to pine for the child who may never be conceived or finally having the nerve to change careers or become self-employed rather than staying in a dead-end job that offers no recognition for accomplishments. The key is understanding that there is a time for everything. Therefore, there is a time to patiently endure and a time to stop enduring and get busy with the resolving.

> *Patience is power; with time and patience the mulberry leaf becomes silk.*
> CHINESE PROVERB

---

1. Jane Austen, *Emma*, The Complete Novels of Jane Austen, vol. II (New York: The Modern Library, 1992), pp. 313-14, 316.

2. Ibid., p. 297.

3. Ibid., p. 313.

Love is kind...

~ 2 ~

Fanny Price and the Queen of Mean

*Kindness is a language the dumb can speak and
the deaf can hear and understand.*
~ CHRISTIAN NESTELL BOVEE ~

One of the most despicable characters in all of Jane Austen's
novels is Aunt Norris in *Mansfield Park*. That woman is a cold-
hearted, mean-spirited, self-centered, old bat. And if that's not
enough, she's not very nice either! Unfortunately I've met a few
people in the real world just like her—and I'm sure you have too.

Equally unfortunate is the fact that sometimes "Aunt Norris"
is sitting on a church pew. I "fondly" remember Dora, who was
rabidly self-centered—and that was on a good day. Dora thrived
on conflict and could barely carry on a conversation without
bashing someone. And there were the mean-spirited barbs she
always threw at people. Those jabs were usually delivered in a

23

soft tone and with a smile so the victim would go away thinking, "Surely she didn't mean that the way it sounded." But, oh, how much she did mean what she said…and a whole lot more she didn't say!

On top of everything else, Dora was so insecure she couldn't stand the thought of another woman outshining her in any way. Therefore she believed it was her responsibility to tear down the talented and beautiful females in her sphere. If subtle attacks didn't work, she moved to more hostile verbal assaults and character-smashing slander. It didn't matter if the female under attack had served and befriended her, Dora had to take the woman down.

Dora was a female barracuda. I have a hunch when Jane Austen created Aunt Norris, it was out of personal experience. These type of people have existed for generations and, unfortunately, will continue to exist as the years unfold.

Aunt Norris is the antithesis of Fanny Price. *Wow!* What a woman Fanny is! When Austen crafted her, she created a character who shines as a person of kindness and wisdom. Fanny might as well have wings and a halo. She even manages to snare the attention of Henry Crawford, who wouldn't know good principles if they bit him on the nose. Even he recognizes something remarkable about Fanny:

> *Fanny's beauty of face and figure, Fanny's graces of manner and goodness of heart, were the exhaustless theme. The gentleness, modesty, and sweetness of her character were warmly*

expatiated on, that sweetness which makes so essential a part of every woman's worth in the judgment of man...Her temper he had good reason to depend on and to praise...Then, her understanding was beyond every suspicion, quick and clear; and her manners were the mirror of her own modest and elegant mind. Nor was this all. Henry Crawford had too much sense not to feel the worth of good principles in a wife, though he was too little accustomed to serious reflection to know them by their proper name; but when he talked of her having such a steadiness and regularity of conduct, such a high notion of honour, and such an observance of decorum as might warrant any man in the fullest dependence on her faith and integrity, he expressed what was inspired by the knowledge of her being well principled and religious.[1]

When I think of Fanny, I'm reminded of Cinderella, who meekly slaves away under the abuse of her wicked stepmother and stepsisters. Like Cinderella, Fanny begins the story as nothing more than a poor relation of the Bertrams, who view her as a second-class servant rather than a true family member. At the end of the fairy tale, Cinderella gains a prince but never reconciles with her stepmother and stepsisters. Fortunately, Jane Austen presents Fanny with a better outcome. While she certainly wins Edmund, her own Prince Charming, by the book's ending she has also risen to a place of honor with the Bertrams...or at least she's the queen bee anyway.

According to the book of Galatians, we reap what we sow (6:7). That principle pays off big for Fanny. After years of being mistreated and sometimes abused in the face of her selfless service and kindness, the Bertrams awaken to see Fanny for what she is: a very wise queen bee waiting to happen. Joseph Joubert, a French moralist, stated, "Kindness is loving people more than they deserve." Fanny Price, of all Austen's heroines, deserves the title of "Most Kind."

Would that we all could model her ability to live out love through kindness. Luke 6 could easily be Fanny's theme chapter for life. Verses 27-28 and 35-36 reveal Jesus' words: "But I tell you who hear me: Love your enemies, do good to those who hate you, bless those who curse you, pray for those who mistreat you....Then your reward will be great, and you will be sons of the Most High, because he is kind to the ungrateful and wicked. Be merciful, just as your Father is merciful."

As Fanny Price lives out the principles in these verses, she manifests a truth that some never learn. If you don't *feel* love, screw up all the courage you have and *live* love anyway. While our attitudes often affect our actions, our actions will definitely affect our attitudes. Acting out kindness to our enemies is a good way to experience God's love toward them.

I believe Jane Austen, a minister's daughter, fully understood this as she unfolded these truths in her heroine's life and decorated the novel with *shades of kindness*. Fanny's individual generosities are so numerous they could fill this book, but each of these acts is colored with nuances from Scripture. Given this observation, it's undisputable that Fanny manifests four major kindnesses found in Luke 6. She 1) does good to those who despise her,

2) blesses those who curse her, 3) is kind to the wicked, and 4) is merciful, just as her heavenly Father is merciful.

As you consider Fanny's many kindnesses, challenge yourself to follow her example. Think about the tough relationships with those who are ungrateful, maybe even hateful. Picture that person's face in your mind, and I don't mean on the dartboard, either! Ask yourself how you can model Fanny's kind heart with those dart-worthy people in your life.

> *The best portion of a good man's life is his little, nameless, unremembered acts of kindness and of love.*
> ~ WILLIAM WORDSWORTH ~

Kindness #1: Fanny does good to those who despise her

Let me tell you about Lynda. She was born with a remarkable combination of blessings. She grew into an attractive lady with a good figure, outgoing personality, and considerable musical talent. She was also academically brilliant and achieved a high education with honors. She possessed an uncanny ability to make and manage money, so eventually Lynda emerged from a poverty-stricken childhood into more and more promises of wealth. She also worked hard and didn't mind paying her dues and putting feet to her visions and dreams.

Aside from all these attributes, Lynda was a generous person who loved people. She cared for the elderly and children and often served those who were less fortunate. She was a woman of God…a woman of great passion…a woman who loved without constraint.

Lynda's main problem was that she was also somewhat naive. She made the mistake of assuming that others loved with the same abandon as she…others whom she served…others like Dora and Aunt Norris. In her mind and heart she would never plot to harm a soul, and she erroneously assumed most people were the same. Unfortunately, some of the very ones she assumed this about were so eaten up with jealousy and dislike they tore her down when given half a chance.

From the first of *Mansfield Park,* Aunt Norris views it as her responsibility to tear down Fanny. If anything good happens Norris wants to take credit for it. If anything bad happens she prefers to blame Fanny. Never does Aunt Norris show Fanny any affection or consideration—not even when the girl is a mere child and moving into the home of relatives who are total strangers.

The tragic fact is that Fanny is Norris' own flesh and blood. Norris' overactive sense of class-consciousness outweighs the bonds of close blood relations. She blatantly heaps verbal abuse upon her niece and never attempts to apologize. Equally mind-boggling is Fanny's response. Never once as a child or adult does she erupt in rage at Aunt Norris or throw a temper tantrum in which she demands a thing.

As Fanny grows up, her Aunt Norris never changes. And aside from physical maturation, Fanny doesn't change much outwardly. But inwardly, she begins to exhibit a strong sense of balance and sound judgment…or at least a ream or two of common sense. Unfortunately, Norris, that blind-as-a-bat ninny, never recognizes this. She begins their relationship with condescending admonitions and so continues throughout the novel. In the end she even blames Fanny—an innocent bystander—for Henry Crawford and Maria Bertram's illicit affair.

Nevertheless, Fanny shows respect to Aunt Norris. She does good to the woman who despises her. Fanny's service to Norris is best illustrated when she cuts roses for Lady Bertram in the heat, then walks twice to Mrs. Norris' house. The result is a horrific, heat-induced headache for Fanny. When Edmund challenges both his aunts over their treatment of Fanny, Norris acts as if Fanny is nothing but a workhorse and her sacrifice is to be expected.

Even though Fanny doesn't reap what she sows with Norris, she does with Edmund. From the very minute Edmund realizes Fanny's service and sacrifice, he begins to serve *her*. He chastises his aunt and mother for overexposing Fanny to the sun. Next he brings Fanny a glass of Madeira and tells her to drink most of it. He further decides she must have regular access to her horse, despite disappointing Miss Crawford, who has been riding Fanny's horse for days.

As with Fanny, rest assured that no matter who in your life is that "wonderful witch," aka "Aunt Norris," and how many times you feel that your kindnesses are unnoticed and unappreciated, you will reap what you sow. God is watching. He will repay you, even if He uses someone else to do it.

Kindness #2: Fanny blesses those who curse her

After years of trusting Dora, Lynda finally awakened to the fact that Dora wasn't the friend she posed as. Lynda's first hint came when Dora verbally bashed her for a trivial matter. From there, Lynda took a hard look at herself and at the other females in her life who, like Dora, felt compelled to attack her. She realized just how naive she'd been. She'd spent her whole youth not understanding that when a woman is "cursed" with beauty and brilliance while being kind and loving, she is considered an open target for other women who are driven by jealousy.

She sadly realized that through the years many people had despised her kindhearted attempts at friendship. She began to evaluate one situation after another and came to a sickening understanding. In the past, she'd erroneously assumed she was being attacked because of something she'd done wrong, which caused her to become depressed. After all, the attackers always implied such. But in reality, she'd done nothing wrong. She'd really been attacked simply because she was being who she was created to be and those like Dora despised her for it.

Even though these dynamics exist today, female competition is as old as the human race. While many people claim that males are more competitive than females, the truth is that female competition against other females can be just as volatile and, with those like Dora, subtly wicked. In 1800 England, the competition revolved around the very survival of those women competing for husbands.

When *Mansfield Park* was written (in 1814), a woman without a monetary fortune held no option for livelihood other than marriage. The laws of England prohibited women—even wealthy women—from inheriting or owning property, and no "decent" woman worked in public. If a man had only female offspring, then at his death his property went, not to his wife or daughters, but to the next male relative...even if he was a distant cousin they barely knew. This dynamic plays a major role in *Pride and Prejudice, Sense and Sensibility,* and *Mansfield Park.*

Therefore, when a single woman of low fortune, or no fortune, rejected a wealthy suitor, she was turning down her only chance at a livelihood or having a home to call her own. If she remained single, and was fortunate, she lived with her father. At her father's death, a single woman would often live with a male relative or subsist on whatever money she inherited. For some, rejecting a marriage proposal was the equivalent to embracing dire poverty. Any young lady of low fortune or no fortune who turned down a well-to-do man's proposal was viewed as nuts—especially by other females who might be as envious of her as Dora was of Lynda.

Fanny Price is no exception. When Henry Crawford proposes to Fanny, everyone expects her to accept. After all, she is as poor as dirt with no line of suitors waiting. In light of the social plight of women in nineteenth-century England, Fanny Price's rejection of Henry's proposal is nothing short of courageous and strong, especially when she won't budge in the face of her Uncle Tom's disapproval—and she's scared stiff of Uncle Tom.

> *"Am I to understand," said Sir Thomas, after a few moments' silence, "that you mean to refuse Mr. Crawford?"*
>
> *"Yes, sir."*
>
> *"Refuse him?"*
>
> *"Yes, sir."*
>
> *"Refuse Mr. Crawford! Upon what plea? For what reason?"*
>
> *"I—I cannot like him, sir, well enough to marry him."*
>
> *"This is very strange!" said Sir Thomas, in a voice of calm displeasure. "There is something in this which my comprehension does not reach. Here is a young man wishing to pay his addresses to you with everything to recommend him....It is of no use, I perceive, to talk to you. We had better put an end to this most mortifying conference."[2]*

In the midst of his astonishment, Sir Thomas berates Fanny in a way that would make Aunt Norris, Dora, and all their kindred spirits proud. Among other things, he tells Fanny she has destroyed his good opinion of her and that she selfishly thinks of herself with no regard for how marrying a rich man can help her poor family. If that tongue-lashing isn't enough, he also accuses her of being willful and perverse.

Overall, Sir Thomas comes as close to blatantly cursing Fanny as Dora did Lynda. But through it all, Fanny never wavers from such respectful responses as "Yes, sir" and "No, sir." Early in the conversation, Fanny also blesses Sir Thomas by not mentioning the outlandish behavior of his own daughters, who shamelessly compete for Henry Crawford—particularly Maria, an engaged woman. Of course, Henry is a willing participant in the scandalous flirtations. By the time Sir Thomas has all but called Fanny a filthy wench, she bursts into tears.

Even after this awful conversation, Fanny never once shows anything but respect toward her uncle. She is a true example of one who lives kindness by blessing those who curse her. But notice that in all her kindnesses, Fanny refuses to compromise her standards or go against her heart. Remember, according to the law, Fanny has no means to support herself. Her only deliverance from a horrid state of poverty is marriage to a man of fortune. But she never bends in her resolve not to marry Henry—even in the face of bold scorn and the family's pressure to marry him.

Fanny's love for integrity is much greater than pleasing her family or even her need for livelihood. She does not confuse blessing those who curse her with pleasing people or compromising standards. She never ignores morals or negates truth. Like Christ when He encountered the adulterous woman at the well, Fanny adheres to truth while extending mercy.

Kindness #3: Fanny is kind to the wicked

The realization that she wasn't at fault sank into Lynda and changed everything. Her naiveté vanished, and when meeting new people she expected the same dynamics that once confused her. When jealous women attacked or despised her, she saw the problem for what it really was. She was no longer taken by surprise. She also learned to draw some boundaries with those who were jealous. Lynda came to understand that she could never have a healthy relationship with Dora or those like her.

I wonder how Mary Crawford would have acted if she knew Fanny was in love with Edmund? I'm certain she probably would have treated Fanny like Dora treated Lynda. She would have been engulfed in a tide of jealousy, bared her teeth, snarled, and gone for Fanny's jugular vein.

When I wrote *Central Park* (based on *Mansfield Park*), I created a scenario that Jane Austen did not. Carrie Casper is my modern interpretation of Austen's Mary Crawford. Carrie is just as much an immoral socialite as the original Mary. However, I have her gradually realize that Ethan Summers (my Edmund) is in love with Francine Ponce (my Fanny). The dynamic grows until Carrie confronts Ethan:

>*"You're in love with her, aren't you?"…*
>
>*"No," Ethan said and thought he was telling the truth. But with his denial came the conviction that he didn't understand his own heart.*
>
>*"You're lying!"…Carrie ran in place and screamed like a wild woman. "I have been an idiot," she roared. "I see the way you look at her…the way you protect her…the way she looks at you. I suspected it from the start, but I talked myself out of it."*
>
>*Ethan staggered backward. Each of Carrie's claims hit him in the gut like a physical punch. He stopped when he slammed*

*into the wall. And Ethan finally understood that his attraction
for Francine wasn't a sick fascination.*

*It was love. It was pure love. And it was perfectly natural
and perfectly honorable.*[3]

This interaction occurs after Ethan realizes that Carrie is a
female version of her sleazy brother, Hugh. Francine recognizes
Hugh and Carrie for what they are from the first meeting.
Likewise, Fanny Price sees through Miss Crawford from their
early acquaintance.

Like my Carrie Casper, Mary Crawford is not much better
than her brother, Henry, that low-moraled, moneyed scoundrel
who proposes to Fanny and eventually runs off with the newly
married Maria. All through the novel, Mary's words reveal her
true colors, and those colors are anything but pure. On top of
that, they're all wrong! She not only has twisted morals, but
she also slams churches and the clergy—until she finds out
Edmund's career choice.

Fanny's reactions throughout the book reveal her true character. Initially, she is as angry with Mary's verbal attack against
the clergy as Edmund is uncomfortable with it. But as Edmund's
sister, Julia, announces that Edmund is soon to become a clergyman, Fanny's anger subsides. When Mary "looked almost aghast
under the new idea she was receiving, Fanny pitied her. 'How
distressed she will be at what she said just now,' passed across her
mind."[4] It's a rare and special lady who can earnestly pity her rival.
While Mary is using her feminine wiles to snare the man Fanny

loves, Fanny still feels sorry for the vixen. Never once does Fanny ever do anything but show Mary friendship and respect.

Many people in Fanny's situation would have slapped Mary, grabbed Edmund by the ears, and hollered, "Mary's a shameless hussy and the *last* woman you need to marry!" But not Fanny. I seriously doubt the word "hussy" would ever leave Fanny's lips. Instead of striking out at Mary, Fanny Price quietly offers her kindness while silently allowing the situation to unfold. She gives Edmund the freedom to come to his own conclusions about Mary's twisted and somewhat wicked value system. Ironically, Mary Crawford turns out to be everything Sir Thomas accuses Fanny of being.

In the end, Fanny has nothing to apologize for because she has lived kindness and love even in the face of a heart-rending situation. The moral? If you do your best to be kind, you will have fewer regrets…and have to apologize much less.

Kindness #4: Fanny is merciful, just as her heavenly Father is merciful

By the end of *Mansfield Park* Fanny has been abused, mistreated, disrespected, verbally attacked, told she is self-centered, and blamed for Henry and Maria's sin. Washington Irving states, "A kind heart is a fountain of gladness, making everything in its vicinity freshen into smiles." That is exactly what finally happens with Fanny Price. Almost everyone in the Bertram household finally comes to their senses and realizes that they were wrong in their treatment of her—everyone, except Aunt Norris, who is so emotionally and spiritually bereft she wouldn't recognize the angel Gabriel if he whacked her over the head with a golden scepter.

When Fanny reenters the Bertram household after the visit with her family of origin, she is welcomed with opened-arms as a daughter who has an important place in the home and family. By her wisdom and acts of kindness she reverses her lot in life and becomes the symbol of honor and respect to the Bertrams. Interestingly enough, Fanny never once says "I told you so." She never harbors resentment toward the Bertrams or fumes because of their former ill treatment. Instead she extends the very mercy she receives from her heavenly Father and revels in the love the Bertrams bestow upon her.

Gradually, one other member of the Bertram household awakens to his romantic love for Fanny. Edmund goes from having only "Fanny's friendship…to cling to"[5] to "ceasing to care about Miss Crawford, and becoming as anxious to marry Fanny as Fanny herself could desire."[6] The first Bertram to show Fanny kindness as a child is the one who is wooed by her own kindness as an adult. And Fanny extends Edmund as much mercy as she does his family. She forgives him for his folly in being duped by Mary Crawford, embraces him, and finds marital fulfillment in his arms.

Any time we have been falsely accused or mistreated, we can be tempted to dish out the abuse that has been meted us. While returning abuse for abuse is never appropriate, absolute honesty and drawing boundaries is. Notice that in all her kindnesses, Fanny had her limits. Even though she is friendly to Mary Crawford, she never lies to herself about what Mary is. And even though she respects her Uncle Tom, she refuses to sell herself to Henry Crawford just to please him.

Just as Lynda drew boundaries with Dora, we need to learn that living Christ is a gutsy undertaking that involves knowing when to draw lines and when to remain silent. Sometimes Jesus overturned tables. Other times, He didn't respond at all. Often He rebuked his critics. But then He sometimes ignored them as well. He never negated truth and called some folks hypocrites and vipers. And when everything was said and done, He extended the greatest kindness of all: He died for everyone. Only through wisdom can we discern what to do and when to do it while always maintaining kindness of heart.

As my father told me: "Debra, it never hurts to be nice."

> *You cannot do a kindness too soon, for you never know how soon it will be too late.*
> ~ RALPH WALDO EMERSON ~

1. Jane Austen, *Mansfield Park*, The Complete Novels of Jane Austen, vol. I (New York: The Modern Library, 1992), pp. 766-67.

2. Ibid., pp. 780-82

3. Debra White Smith, *Central Park* (Eugene, OR: Harvest House, 2005), p. 327.

4. Austen, *Mansfield Park*, p. 618.

5. Ibid., p. 888.

6. Ibid., p. 895.

Love does not envy...

$\sim$ 3 $\sim$

Henry Crawford and the Slime Sisters

And oft, my jealousy shapes faults that are not.
$\sim$ William Shakespeare $\sim$

Within the last year my husband and I purchased a new ministry headquarters. The property includes a residence for us as well as a ministry building and conference grounds. When we bought the property, it had been on the market for about two years and had not been maintained well by the owner. The huge pool had been emptied and left as a rain trap. As a result, the rain built up in the pool and created a wonderful community for reptiles and amphibians. That's a really nice way of saying the deep end of the pool looked like a green, slimy pond full of frogs and snakes. When my husband began cleaning out the pool, we discovered there was an all-out frog-fest on. Those critters abounded! By the time he finished the job, he'd also encountered some harmless snakes. Daniel and our son worked like crazy to get the pool pressure-washed and cleaned.

Then we filled the pool with water, poured in the chemicals, and the fun began.

However, the reptile and amphibian community failed to send out notices to all former visitors that the pool was no longer a haven for critters. The first couple of months the pool was up and running, we found snakes near the pool. We also never knew when we awoke every morning whether or not the pool would be full of unsuspecting frogs, who were expecting the pond experience and wound up sinking into chlorinated pool water. Chlorine kills frogs. We were a frog graveyard for dozens of them. Finally word must have gotten out because the dead frog phenomenon subsided. The frogs, however, still hang around. The kids continue to find dead and living frogs in and on the slide.

This brings up an interesting life principle. If we aren't careful, our hearts and minds can become as slimy with negativity as the pool was. From there, we can become infested with defeating thought patterns that are as nasty as swamp frogs and as fork-tongued as serpents. One of those patterns is envy.

When Jane Austen created the Bertram sisters in *Mansfield Park*, she crafted women who would be right at home in my pond-pool. I give them the "Slime Sisters Award." These sisters are so eaten up with trying to best each other for Henry Crawford's attention that they stop just short of mud wrestling. According to old-time politician Job E. Hedges, "Lots of people know a good thing the minute the other fellow sees it first." Such is the case with Maria and Julia Bertram.

These two sisters take one look at Henry Crawford and decide he's plain. The second encounter proves him less plain. And the third time they meet "he was no longer allowed to be called [plain] by anybody. He was, in fact, the most agreeable young man the sisters had ever known, and they were equally delighted with him."[1] Before long, both sisters decide they've got to have him—or at least beat the other out of getting him.

> *Wednesday was fine, and soon after breakfast the barouche arrived, Mr. Crawford driving his sisters; and as everybody was ready, there was nothing to be done but for Mrs. Grant to alight, and the others to take their places. The place of all places, the envied seat, the post of honour, was unappropriated. To whose happy lot was it to fall? While each of the Miss Bertrams were meditating how best, and with the most appearance of obliging the others, to secure it, the matter was settled by Mrs. Grant's saying, as she stepped from the carriage, "As there are five of you, it will be better that one should sit with Henry; and as you were saying lately that you wished you could drive, Julia, I think this will be a good opportunity for you to take a lesson."*
>
> *Happy Julia! Unhappy Maria! The former was on the barouche-box in a moment, the latter took her seat within, in gloom and mortification; and the carriage drove off amid the good wishes of the two remaining ladies, and the barking of pug in his mistress's arms.[2]*

Julia and Maria remind me of two hummingbirds fighting for territory. Those beautiful, seemingly innocent creatures ruthlessly guard their territory like gladiators with beaks. Before the Bertram sisters have known Henry long, they are in a frenzied fit of competition over who gets to monopolize him. Henry, the shallow egotist, loves every minute of it and encourages the ladies to fight over him all they will. The Bertram sisters shamelessly oblige him. They fall into a round of rivalry that nearly turns into an all-out cat fight. Both are engulfed in envy, strife, and a battle of the wills and words that can't be ignored. During their competition for Henry, the sisters exhibit the symptoms of envy that transcend time and culture. They *covet something, compete for territory,* and *attack to secure territory.*

These symptoms are not limited to two sisters in Jane Austen's novel. They appear in modern life in everyday relationships among friends, professionals, and yes, even sisters and other relatives. According to Francois de la Rochefoucauls, "In jealousy there is more of self-love than love to another." In *Mansfield Park,* Mary Crawford states, "Selfishness must always be forgiven you know, because there is no hope of a cure."[3]

The Bertram sisters blatantly manifest jealousy as well as self-love, but these traits aren't always so easily recognized...especially in ourselves. If you find traces of this green-eyed monster lurking in your mind, ask yourself how it might be harming your relationships and how you might be bettered by arranging the monster's execution.

> O, *beware, my Lord, of jealousy; It is the green-eyed*
> *monster which doth mock the meat it feeds on.*
> ~ WILLIAM SHAKESPEARE ~

Coveting

Coveting occurs when a person would take something or beat another out of something if given the opportunity. Through the years I have heard numerous stories about sisters who were estranged because of one coveting something the other has. One may be envious over a great figure, beauty, intellect, possessions, or position. The envy spawns covetous thoughts, and even if no outward action is ever manifested, in the heart one sister has taken from the other. Sometimes the scenario involves brothers. I've known of one brother having to file bankruptcy while the other—his partner in business—did everything he could to force his sibling out of business.

And don't think mothers and fathers are exempt. I have known of mothers who have become so jealous of their own daughters that they abuse them, force them into abusive relationships, or abandon them. I've heard of fathers who were so threatened by their own sons that they competed with them and wouldn't dare encourage and empower them.

Jane Austen obviously recognized that envy and jealousy exist among families because her portrayal of the Bertram sisters is so realistic. In *Mansfield Park*, Julia and Maria covet a living, breathing specimen of masculinity. Forget that these two ladies have the same bloodline, have grown up together, and are supposed to love each other. When they each desire Henry Crawford, their sisterhood is ignored.

As for Henry, he decides he likes Maria best. After all, she is the most attractive. She is also engaged, and he admits to liking her better because of it. This foreshadows all sorts of forbidden flirtation.

Henry Crawford has a reputation for flirtation. Mary Crawford tells her sister, "I have three very particular friends who have been all dying for him in their turn; and the pains which they, their mothers (very clever women), as well as my dear aunt and myself, have taken to reason, coax, or trick him into marrying, is inconceivable! He is the most horrible flirt that can be imagined. If your Miss Bertrams do not like to have their hearts broke, let them avoid Henry."[4] From this point on the Miss Bertrams emotionally writhe with each other, trying to outwit the other in an effort to snare Henry.

Ironically, we seldom hear anyone admit to envy. Usually when the problem involves relatives, the envious one projects blame for the whole problem upon the one envied. False accusations are often part of the ugly process. If the jealous person is a friend or acquaintance with the one envied, he or she may say something like, "I don't like that person," when in reality it's not dislike they're feeling, it's envy. And usually, it all boils down to the fact that they want what the disliked party has: recognition, attention, career, power…or even that person's boyfriend or wife.

Competing for Territory

Coveting often drives its victim to competition. The envious thought process usually goes like this, "I want what the other person has, and I'll beat him out of it the first chance I get." From there, the contest begins. While this mind-set might be healthy in checkers and ice hockey, it ruins relationships—especially if a friend or relative is coming after you with a hockey stick. Often the competition between siblings starts in early childhood and plagues them for life. For the Bertram sisters, this tug-of-war is blatant when they try to outwit each other over who will sit by Henry in his barouche during the ride to the Rushworth estate.

Their competition escalates upon their arrival at Sotherton. After scandalously flirting with each other, Maria and Henry decide to squeeze through an opening in a gate and walk together alone…completely alone. *Whoa!* In nineteenth-century England, this is nearly as risqué as a weekend fling. Fanny Price, who witnesses the whole thing, is certainly aghast. And Jane Austen emphasizes the indecency by using the gate imagery. Henry and Maria should be constrained by propriety and the fact that she is engaged, but they squeeze through physical and social mores and burst into inappropriate territory.

Once Julia walks upon the scene and realizes her sister has scored a point in monopolizing Henry, she is exasperated. When Fanny tries to convince Julia to wait on Rushworth and not to follow Henry and Maria through the gate, she declares, "*That* is Miss Maria's concern. I am not obliged to punish myself for *her* sins."[5]

The contest intensifies as the plot unfolds. Later in the novel, both sisters pine for the role of Henry's female counterpart, Agatha, in a home-based play production of *Lover's Vows.* But as with the gate scene, Maria wins the round again when Henry beseeches Julia *not* to take the role of Agatha because she is not serious enough to successfully play the woeful part. From this Julia realizes she can trust neither Henry nor her sister.

As with most situations where people are driven by envy, Julia and Maria are pouring their energies into outwitting each other. Often, in the real world, this self-absorbed process can blind us to needs around us or more worthy goals. Perhaps that's why Galatians 5 labels envy and jealousy as "acts of the sinful nature." There's nothing more self-centered than subordinating and demoralizing another in order to get what you want. This is the antithesis of love.

Attacking to Secure Territory

Lucky is a male cat we adopted years ago when I found him stranded in the middle of a busy road. At the time he was only about three weeks old. We've pampered him since the moment we got him. I even bought special kitten formula at the vet for him when he was a baby.

He's grown into quite a feline with an attitude. Even though he's been neutered, he believes he has to jealously guard the entire yard against other male cats. He loves nothing more than spending the night outside, defending his territory and daring any other tomcat to cross into his yard. Since he's got such an in-your-face strut, I've seen him intimidate cats half again as big as he is. And he doesn't mind attacking to enforce that *he rules!*

In the house, Lucky tries to rule as severely as he does in the yard—and that means everyone in our family is his royal subject. If one of us walks by while he's lounging on the floor and he's not in the mood to be walked by, he'll growl and swat at us. Sometimes, if he's really crabby, he'll even show his "vampire teeth" and hiss with a "don't cross me" look in his eyes. Frankly, I'm thinking we should change his name to Hitler.

Even though our whole family laughs at Lucky, such behavior isn't so funny when it's manifested by humans. And human beings *do* stake their territory and *will* attack to protect it. While Julia Bertram appears to be a piteous character when Henry blatantly chooses Maria for the part in the play, Julia has already savored her moments of attack. Just like my cat contends with his rivals, so Julia moves from a few subtle stabs at Maria to full-blown competition.

On the way to Sotherton, when Julia wins the coveted seat by Henry, she's not satisfied with mere victory. She's driven to taunt her sister. After Maria grows irritated over having lost the spot by Henry, Julia shamelessly gloats and throws verbal darts at Maria. And Julia doesn't stop there. Later, when they enter the chapel at Sotherton, she launches another round of verbal barbs by emphasizing to Henry that her sister is engaged to Rushworth: "Julia called Mr. Crawford's attention to her sister, by saying, 'Do look at Mr. Rushworth and Maria, standing side by side, exactly as if the ceremony were going to be performed.

Have not they completely the air of it?"[6] In other words, "Na-na-aaa na-naaaa-na! You're already engaged, and Henry can be all mine!"

Before the book is over, both sisters have done their share of attacking each other. When it comes to Henry Crawford, neither would win the award for Miss Congeniality. Both feel too insecure in their position with Henry to allow the other access to him. Too many times, envy exists because of the very deep-rooted problems Maria and Julia manifest: feelings of inadequacy, insecurity, and a sense of lacking something.

Regardless of how Julia competes or attacks, she winds up the loser in vying for Henry's favoritism and attention. In the end he and Maria run off together, *after* she's already married Rushworth. And despite the fact that Austen wrote *Mansfield Park* in the early nineteenth century, when conservative views abounded, she makes it very clear that Maria and Henry aren't out picking daisies. They live together and have a high old time—until they start fighting, that is. Then the two break up, which leaves Maria a scandalized outcast who must move abroad with her Aunt Norris, that "wonderful," old-bat-of-a-relative who could exasperate a corpse.

Which leads to the wretched truth about envy and the competitive attacks that go with it: Sometimes the very thing you long for and fight for can be your downfall.

> *Jealousy is...a tiger that tears not only its prey but also its own raging heart.*
> ~ MICHAEL BEER ~

1. Jane Austen, *Mansfield Park*, The Complete Novels of Jane Austen, vol. I (New York: The Modern Library, 1992), p. 585.

2. Ibid., pp. 612-13.

3. Ibid., p. 603.

4. Ibid., p. 584.

5. Ibid., p. 627.

6. Ibid., p. 619.

Love does not boast...

Augusta Elton and the Stinky Cloud

As a rule, there is no surer way to the dislike of men than to behave well where they have behaved badly.
~ LEW WALLACE ~

Emma was not required, by any subsequent discovery, to retract her ill opinion of Mrs. Elton. Her observation had been pretty correct. Such as [Augusta] Elton appeared to her on this second interview, such she appeared whenever they met again: self-important, presuming, familiar, ignorant, and ill-bred. She had a little beauty and a little accomplishment, but so little judgment that she thought herself coming with superior knowledge of the world, to enliven and improve a country neighbourhood.[1]

Augusta Elton. I've declared her the "Most Boastful." How many people have you met like her? I wouldn't be surprised to find her in the dictionary as a definitive answer to the word "boast." The woman can't open her mouth without oozing about how wonderful she is and how she's going to add culture to Emma Woodhouse's neighborhood. Augusta reminds me of a used car salesman, dressed in an obnoxious striped blazer, trying to sell clunkers he claims are jewels. Augusta is trying to sell herself. Despite her over-inflated opinion of herself, she's a "clunker," and she'll never be half as jewel-like as she believes. "There are no people that are quite so vulgar as the over-refined," says Mark Twain. And Augusta Elton qualifies as "over-refined." She's a self-proclaimed socialite who gets her value from a brother-in-law who's supposed to own a wide stretch of property.

By the end of *Emma*, I'd like to sentence Augusta to a deserted island with Aunt Norris from *Mansfield Park*, and let the two of them suffocate each other with their stuffy social airs. And that's usually the reaction most people have to boasters like Augusta. We're often tempted to cut them down to size…or at least send them on a slow boat to China. We ask,

> Why does she think she's so great, anyway?
> Who died and left her queen?
> I'd rather eat a rabid skunk than sit through a meal with her!
> What is your deal, woman!
> Ever thought of washing a few feet? Might do ya good!

Most of the time we don't verbalize these thoughts, especially if we're trying to be nice. Instead, we act like Emma does with Augusta: We paste on a stiff smile and pretend politeness while planning to avoid this obnoxious person for the rest of our lives—even if that means *we* take the slow boat to China. Anything is better than enduring a conversation focused on why the other party is so great and superior to the rest of the world.

Nobody likes a boaster. Nobody. Which leads me to doubt the sanity of anyone who boasts. Do these people really think the rest of the world will be impressed? Do they realize the effect they're having? I believe the answer to that lies in the cause of the boasting.

Frankly, boasting falls into a variety of categories that are caused by different catalysts. Some, like Augusta boast because of *self-importance*. Others might boast due to *insecurity*, which creates a totally different dynamic. And finally, I'm convinced some people may come across as boasters, when in reality they are innocently excited about something new that they want to share with the world. From that vantage, insecure and envious people who observe them usually accuse them of purposefully boasting, even though that's not their heart's intent. These people are *innocent boasters*.

> *To be a man's own fool is bad enough; but the vain man is everybody's.*
> ~ WILLIAM PENN ~

The Self-Important Boaster

Years ago when I realized that inferiority can make people

boast, I began to think that all boasters were trying to hide feelings of inferiority. But then I met a few people like Brenda. I'd admired Brenda from afar and was excited to meet her. When I approached her and introduced myself, she extended her hand and condescended to offer a limp handshake. She was taller than I and looked down her nose at my inferior self. I was disgusted, to say the least. All my excitement over meeting her evaporated. And I decided I didn't care if I never said another word to her. I relieved her of my presence, which I'm sure she never even noticed.

Once I met enough people like Brenda, I realized that there are some people who really believe they are better than everyone else. Furthermore, this type of person seems to attract others just like them. Then they sit around together in their stinky cloud of superiority and wonder why the rest of the world can't be as good as they are.

Self-important boasters carry an attitude with them everywhere they go. Like the character Pigpen in the Charlie Brown cartoon series, they are surrounded by a cloud of dirt. The self-important boaster's cloud is made up of conceit and condescension. Even though this cloud can't be smelled with the physical nose, it can be smelled by our spirits.

When I wrote *Amanda*, based on *Emma*, I made my version of Augusta Elton as obnoxious and smelly as the original. Then I upped her obnoxious rating a rung or two by making her outward appearance as gaudy as her attitude:

*[Sonja Eldridge] enveloped Amanda's hand in both of hers
and squeezed. Amanda glanced down to see enough diamonds
to start a jewelry store. Immediately she wondered if that had
been the purpose of the whole handshake…*

*[Sonja] was wearing enough makeup for two women, and
her dark hair was teased into a frenzied do that made 1950
pageant hair seem small. At closer vantage, Amanda deduced
that the dark hair color probably wasn't Sonja's own. It belonged
to some bottle labeled "Boom Boom Brunette" or something
equally obnoxious…*

*Her blue eyes [were] too bright to be of natural hue and too
cold to be sincere. Amanda deduced Sonja was also wearing
colored contacts and wondered if there was anything about the
woman that wasn't enhanced or teased or plastered.*

*It's a good thing she's got money, Amanda thought and
eyed Sonja's sculptured fingernails, which were long and red and
square. They were every bit as bold as her musky perfume.* Her
grooming bills alone probably cost a fortune. She's like an
oversized poodle![2]

Just as Amanda senses Sonja's boasting nature, so Emma
senses Augusta Elton. The second time Emma encounters
Augusta, she is able to determine her true nature. She became
quite convinced that "Mrs. Elton was a vain woman, extremely
well satisfied with herself, and thinking much of her own
importance; that she meant to shine and be very superior; but
with manners which had been formed in a bad school; pert and
familiar; that all her notions were drawn from one set of people,

and one style of living; that, if not foolish, she was ignorant, and that her society would certainly do Mr. Elton no good."[3] As the novel progresses, Augusta further engrains this impression in the minds of Emma and the reader.

The reason why real love doesn't boast is because self-elevation and boasting are miles removed from the heart of Christ. While the disciples made a major scene over who among them was the greatest, Jesus Christ taught that we must all be servants:

> *Also a dispute arose among them as to which of them was considered to be greatest. Jesus said to them, "The kings of the Gentiles lord it over them; and those who exercise authority over them call themselves Benefactors. But you are not to be like that. Instead, the greatest among you should be like the youngest, and the one who rules like the one who serves. For who is greater, the one who is at the table or the one who serves? Is it not the one who is at the table? But I am among you as one who serves"* (Luke 22:24-27).

While it's very easy to recognize those who haven't adopted an attitude of servanthood, it's just as easy to be tempted to think ourselves above them because of our lack of a boasting spirit. But beware! The first time we start thinking we're above someone who boasts, we become what he or she is.

Insecure Boasters

Insecurity can do wicked things to people. The insecure

person has a continual "recording" playing in his head that says things such as, "You're not of worth. You aren't as good as anyone else. You'll never succeed. People don't like you. And no matter what you do you can't get people to like you." This state of torment can lead people to act and react in ways that may appear bizarre, but they are rooted in the negative recording that never stops filling the person's mind with degrading thoughts about him- or herself. Many times these insecure individuals suffered through a childhood that involved emotional, verbal, physical, or spiritual abuse. Because of this, they've been living in insecurity their whole lives and often don't even realize it.

The insecure person feels inferior. Those feelings of inferiority lead to craving for praise and applause. This often results in overachieving and a soul that pants for recognition. In order to fill this need, insecure people may publicly talk about their accomplishments or praise themselves. This verbal manifestation of their deep need may appear to be rooted in self-important boasting, but it is actually rooted in a frantic desire for affirmation…and for love.

While love doesn't boast because self-elevating boasting is the antithesis of Christ's heart, the heart where love is needed might fall into boasting as a means for begging for love, respect, and appreciation. Where there is a heart overflowing with ample love, there's no tendency toward boasting. Where there is a heart panting for love, the longing can lead to the search for affirmation.

The problem is how do we tell the difference between

someone who is using boasting as a cry for approval and someone who is boasting because he really believes he is superior? You might feel sorry for the insecure boaster and want to minister to him while the haughty boaster is someone you want to avoid. Jane Austen crafted Augusta Elton in a way that leaves little room for questioning that she really does believe she is above everyone else. The clues Austen gives are ones we can use to determine the cause of boasting in others.

The key with Augusta and anyone else boasting from self-elevation lies in what the boasting is centered upon. Augusta's boasting is based on what she is and what she has to offer. It involves the essence of who she is—or the "superior being" she believes she is. A prime example of this occurs in her conversation with Mr. Weston: "I always say a woman cannot have too many resources—and I feel very thankful that I have so many myself as to be quite independent of society."[4] From there she fishes for compliments.

Oh brother! If Augusta Elton were half as wonderful as she thought she was, she wouldn't be so quick to brag because the truly wonderful don't view themselves as better than everyone else. Ironically, neither do insecure boasters.

Unlike the pompous Augusta, the insecure boaster often speaks of accomplishments and goals, rather than innate qualities. Like a toddler who desperately awaits applause for her accomplishments, so goes the insecure. If the toddler is not applauded, she will do whatever she must to grab the parents' attention for an encore. Sadly, some people never have their parents' positive attention, or the encore, and spend their whole lives yearning for applause. So they accomplish…and accomplish…and accomplish…and tell about those accomplishments in a desperate desire to put an end to the demeaning mantra that tortures their spirits. These people really don't believe they are superior to everyone else. Rather, they boast about their superior accomplishments.

Innocent Boasters

Innocent boasters are often energetic people who are positive and excited about life. They may easily attract friends and be popular. They also may be somewhat naive. Because of this naiveté, innocent boasters may not realize how other people perceive them. Many times, they just want to hug the world and be everyone's friend and share the "latest exciting news" about their careers or children or honors they've received. They don't realize in all their "sharing" that the very person they're sharing with is viewing their news as bragging. Too often, the people they share with might be like the Bertram sisters in *Mansfield Park* and be so overcome by envy they are driven to accuse the innocent boaster of vanity.

I believe that the Old Testament story of Joseph is a classic example of a young man who was an innocent boaster. Genesis 37:5-7 states, "Joseph had a dream, and when he told it to his brothers, they hated him all the more. He said to them, 'Listen to this dream I had: We were binding sheaves of grain out in the field when suddenly my sheaf rose and stood upright, while your sheaves gathered around mine and bowed down to it.'" For years I thought Joseph was a self-important boaster based on this featured passage. After all, no person with one shred of common sense would share such a dream with brothers who were already struggling with envy—unless that person was naive and didn't realize the impact of his claims.

I believe that Joseph was indeed so young and so naive that he didn't get that his brothers would despise him when he told them of this dream. His innocence is further shown when he approaches his brothers alone before they stage his death and sell him into slavery. If he suspected how desperately they hated him, he'd have never placed himself in such danger. Later, when Potiphar's wife tries to seduce him, his guileless nature is also revealed in the fact that he allowed himself to be alone with such a lustful woman.

When naive people "boast," they are manifesting a childlike faith that others will be as pleased for them as they are. Like Joseph, they may be pure of heart and often don't understand the complications of peer jealousies. Sometimes they might even be shocked to hear that anyone is jealous of them at all. They often don't understand that a jealousy-driven attack really is about the other person's character problems.

Even though the naive boaster may strike us as a self-elevated boaster, there is a way to discover the cause of the behavior. One of the prime differences between the innocent boaster and the self-elevated boaster is that innocent boasters will also honestly applaud the accomplishments of others. These people are often encouragers who are considered good with other people. They just have this flaw of not understanding how talking too much about their own "exciting news" comes across.

Since Augusta Elton is about as naive as a black mamba, she once again serves as a fantastic contrast for the innocent boaster. When the innocent boaster praises another person, he or she usually means every word and doesn't use the praise as a vehicle for complimenting himself or subtly demeaning the person praised. But even when Augusta appears to be lifting up another, she is actually using the opportunity to brag about herself and subtly demean the person she's praising. In this case, the person is Jane Fairfax:

> *[Jane] is very timid and silent. One can see that she feels the want of encouragement. I like her the better for it. I must confess it is a recommendation to me. I am a great advocate for timidity—and I am sure one does not often meet with it. But in those who are at all inferior it is extremely prepossessing. Oh! I assure you, Jane Fairfax is a very delightful character, and interests me more than I can express.[5]*

In the middle of all her oozing about Jane Fairfax's greatness, Augusta just has to point out that Jane is her social inferior. Furthermore, she also boasts about her possessions and later places herself on equal social standing with Emma Woodhouse.

On a Brag Scale of 1–10, with 10 being the highest, Augusta gets a 50! No wonder Emma nearly throws up every time she gets around her. "'Poor Jane Fairfax!' thought Emma, 'you have not deserved this…This is a punishment beyond what you can have merited. The kindness and protection of Mrs. Elton! "Jane Fairfax and Jane Fairfax!" Heavens! let me suppose that she dares go about Emma Woodhouse-ing me! But, upon my honour, there seems no limits to the licentiousness of that woman's tongue!'"[6]

While Augusta really does have a licentious tongue, most innocent boasters do not. In many ways they are simple in their enthusiasm and want to share with the world. The next time you're tempted to think that an innocent boaster is shamelessly bragging, dare to look past his excitement over "the latest" and see his innocent heart. Have the courage to go ahead and applaud. Most of the time the person honestly doesn't understand how he is coming across. And remember, he'll be the one who will be the most enthusiastic when *you* have good news.

> *The only cure for vanity is laughter, and the only fault that's laughable is vanity.*
> ~ HENRI BERGSON ~

1. Jane Austen, *Emma*, The Complete Novels of Jane Austen, vol. II (New York: The Modern Library, 1992), p. 204.
2. Debra White Smith, *Amanda* (Eugene, OR: Harvest House Publishers, 2006), p. 209.
3. Austen, *Emma*, p. 197.
4. Ibid., p. 224.
5. Ibid., p. 205.
6. Ibid., p. 206.

Love is not proud...

⟳ 5 ⟳

Mr. Darcy and the Not-So-Distressed Damsel

For God does not show favoritism.
~ ROMANS 2:11 ~

About two weeks ago, I attended a Rangers' baseball game near Dallas, Texas. I glanced over my shoulder and noticed an unusual invitation on the huge electronic message board on display for the whole crowd: "Sarah, will you marry me? Love Rick."

I thought, *What a wonderful way to propose! I'm sure Sarah is elated right now.*

Through the years, I've heard of all sorts of creative ways men propose. One guy hired a pilot to fly a banner behind a plane. That banner was a sky-high way to pop the question. Another guy proposed on the popular game show *Deal or No Deal.* Howie Mandell reaffirmed the question to the potential bride with "Deal or no Deal."

Another man knew a police officer. He arranged for his friend the policeman to pull him and his girlfriend over on the side of a main highway. The police officer was very serious and asked both the man and his girlfriend to get out. He told them he was going to have to take them both into the police station but first, he needed the man to remove everything from his pockets. When the guy emptied his pockets, there was a ring box in the mix. At that point, the man proposed. The girlfriend, knowing she'd been creatively tricked, gladly accepted.

Another man had a flight booked with his girlfriend. He boarded the flight early and had the flight attendant pass out a red rose to every passenger who boarded the plane. The guy was notorious for being late. The girlfriend, not knowing he was hiding in the cockpit, worried that he was going to miss the flight.

Before the plane began its taxi, the captain called over the intercom, "There's a young man in the cockpit who wants to pose a special question to a passenger."

Next the future groom's voice came over the intercom with, "Will you marry me?" He then came down the aisle carrying a dozen roses.

Now these are the kinds of proposals that make a woman's heart go pitter-patter. They show that the guy has put a significant amount of thought and planning into the romance. This proves to her that he really cares...that he loves her...that he would do anything in the world for her.

Darcy, in *Pride and Prejudice*, could take a lesson or two from all these Romeos. To say the man's first proposal to Elizabeth is romantically challenged is an understatement. Of all of Jane Austen's heroes, I give him the "Foot in Mouth Award." He firmly plants, not one, but *both* his feet in his mouth, then chews on them a while. His proposal is a classic model for how *not* to ask a woman to marry.

> *After a silence of several minutes, [Darcy] came towards [Elizabeth] in an agitated manner, and thus began:*
>
> *"In vain have I struggled. It will not do. My feelings will not be repressed. You must allow me to tell you how ardently I admire and love you."…He spoke well; but there were feelings besides those of the heart to be detailed, and he was not more eloquent on the subject of tenderness than of pride. His sense of her inferiority—of its being a degradation—of the family obstacles which judgment had always opposed to inclination, were dwelt on with a warmth which seemed due to the consequence he was wounding, but was very unlikely to recommend his suit…*
>
> *He concluded with representing to her the strength of that attachment which, in spite of all his endeavours, he had found impossible to conquer; and with expressing his hope that it would now be rewarded by her acceptance of his hand. As he said this, she could easily see that he had no doubt of a favourable answer. He spoke of apprehension and anxiety, but his countenance expressed real security.[1]*

His offer of marriage in modern language would go something like this, "Elizabeth, I've fallen in love with you despite the fact that you are so far beneath me everyone will wonder if I've lost my mind to even consider marrying you. Your family is an embarrassment to society, and I can't even believe I'm standing here asking you to be my wife. But despite all common sense, here I am anyway." He holds out his arms like he's the best thing to happen to the world. "I'm all yours—despite the fact that I've tried and tried to talk myself out of this. But no matter how I try, I can't convince myself not to love you. Now, do you want to go to Tiffany's to get the ring? Or maybe in your lower-class status, you'd be just as happy with a cubic zirconium from Wal-Mart. I seriously doubt you could tell the difference."

Is it any wonder Elizabeth tells the guy he's a prideful jerk and invites him to get lost—*forever?*

> *Such a circumstance could only exasperate farther, and, when he ceased, the colour rose into her cheeks, and she said:*
>
> *"…I might as well inquire…why with so evident a design of offending and insulting me, you chose to tell me that you liked me against your will, against your reason, and even against your character?…From the very beginning—from the first moment, I may almost say—of my acquaintance with you, your manners, impressing me with the fullest belief of your arrogance, your conceit, and your selfish disdain of the feelings of others, were such as to form that groundwork of disapprobation on which succeeding events have built so immovable a dislike; and I had not known you a month before I felt that you were the last man in the world whom I could ever be prevailed on to marry."[2]*

I am reminded of the old joke many women laughingly toss around: "Nice dress. Too bad it went out of style ten years ago." Just as this is a compliment with a razor-sharp edge, so Darcy's proposal is a compliment with a knife-like stab that pierces Elizabeth's pride. This leads us to the real truth of both Elizabeth and Darcy. They each have their share of pride, and each are deserving of an oversized helping of humble pie.

When Darcy and Elizabeth meet each other, they have met their match. Of all Jane Austen's heroes and heroines, these two stand out as the most electric. The sparks fly from the moment they meet. While each of Austen's stories has special elements that I call my favorite, the Darcy–Elizabeth dynamic wins as my favorite romantic plot. But part of the reason these two characters are so captivating together is that they each have a significant number of issues that repel each other, which creates friction in their budding relationship. The title itself indicates their major issues: *Pride and Prejudice.* And before the book is over, Austen has them both confessing to heaps of each.

Interestingly enough, egocentric pride is a precursor to prejudice and must exist for prejudices to survive. Part of the makeup of prejudices involves negatively judging a group of people as a whole, assigning those negative traits to every person in that group, and then thinking of yourself as better than those people. A prejudiced person pridefully looks down on those upon whom the prejudice is heaped.

Darcy and Elizabeth do their share of this, and each manifests some elements of both pride and prejudice. First Corinthians 13:4 states, "Love is…not proud," and before Darcy and Elizabeth can fully fall in love, they must both recognize that they each have *evidences of pride:* 1) lofty attitude, 2) over-inflated ego, and 3) certainty of being right.

Nobody enjoys being with a person who's manifesting these traits. Like Augusta Elton in *Emma*, we usually want to avoid the prideful however we can. Furthermore, I am convinced pure love cannot and never will coexist with egocentric pride. Even if we don't direct the pride toward the person we love, an over-inflated value of ourselves taints every relationship we have.

> *There was one who thought himself above me, and he*
> *was above me until he had that thought.*
> ~ ELBERT HUBBARD ~

Evidences of Pride

I never cease to be amazed how people with *lofty attitudes* treat people they view as underlings. I recall an incident from years ago that I'll never forget. My husband and I were just moving into a home we'd purchased. Since our new house was larger than our old one, we needed a few new pieces of furniture to fill the gaps. Having always been a bargain maniac and connoisseur of fine garage sales, I cruised the neighborhood for any killer sales that might hold a few unsuspected treasures. Sure enough, I discovered a few antiques that were exactly what we needed.

I also ran into a man with his nose so far in the air I'm sure he'd have drowned if it rained. He barely condescended to sell us his "leftovers." We paid for our antiques and shared a private laugh about how uppity that man was. Granted, he held a respected career position, but he was still far from royalty.

This was years ago when my writing career was just beginning. My son was only one, we hadn't adopted my daughter yet, and I was a stay-at-home mom who was pinching pennies. I'd had only one book and a stack of articles published. I was scheduled to speak at a local event soon after my great garage-sale purchase. A newspaper advertisement came out that weekend announcing I'd be speaking.

A day or so later, my husband and I ran into that garage-sale man who'd not been so humble. Well, guess what! He informed us he'd read the paper and discovered that I was a real, live, honest-to-goodness published author. My oh my did his attitude change! He was so friendly and *so* respectful. Daniel and I were just as kind to him then as we'd been when we first met him, but after we departed from his regal presence, we rolled our eyes.

I said, "If he can't treat me with respect when he thinks I'm a nobody, then why does he think I'm going to believe he really respects me now?"

Daniel agreed.

People who respect others based on wealth or appearance or career alone really don't understand God's priorities. True respect is based upon the fact that the person is a human being created in the image of God. Therefore, everyone is deserving of basic, human respect whether he (or she) is a janitor or a doctor or a schoolteacher. And no one enjoys being viewed as a nobody.

This is a big part of the reason Mr. Darcy didn't win a popularity contest with Elizabeth Bennet. When he first appears in the novel,

> *Mr. Darcy soon drew the attention of the room by his fine, tall person, handsome features, noble mien, and the report which was in general circulation within five minutes after his entrance, of his having ten thousand a year [equivalent to about $300,000–$400,000 in today's dollars]…He was looked on with great admiration for about half the evening, till his manners gave a disgust which turned the tide of his popularity; for he was discovered to be proud; to be above his company, and above being pleased; and not all his large estate in Derbyshire could then save him from having a most forbidding, disagreeable countenance, and being unworthy to be compared with his friend.[3]*

Darcy's lofty attitude hung out all over him and nobody within a mile missed it. The problems are worsened when Bingley tries to get Darcy to dance. At that point he says there's not a woman in the room good enough for him to dance with, including Elizabeth, who isn't pretty enough. This leaves Elizabeth as exasperated at Darcy as I was at the garage-sale man.

And that's the way bad attitudes usually work. Covering them up is like trying to hide the hiccups. They pop out at all the wrong times and reveal themselves whether you realize it or not.

An "I'm better than you" spirit is an aura a person carries, and everyone he encounters can sense it—especially those whom the prideful individual believes are beneath him. Voltaire best sums it up: "The infinitely little have a pride infinitely great."

Darcy's disdain centered upon class consciousness steeped in monetary superiority. While this cancer is still intact in modern times, other reasons for a lofty spirit often afflict us as well. Alleged racial and gender "superiority" permeate our society as salt permeates the sea. Tragically, the church isn't immune from these sinful attitudes. And the reaction to persnickety people is usually the same as what the Bennets and other ball attendees exhibited: Oh gag!

Even though Darcy has an income equivalent to nearly half a million dollars a year, and even though he is handsome and has a "noble mien," once his attitude stank up the room, the crowd drew their own conclusions. The very things Darcy thought gave him high status meant little in that status-conscious crowd. And so it goes with us.

As I already mentioned, last year Daniel and I purchased our new ministry headquarters. I use the word "new" loosely because the home itself is about 70 years old. However, the ministry building is only about 10 years old, as are the grounds' amenities. As with our previous home, this one is larger than the last. So what did we do? We began shopping for furniture. This time the budget wasn't as tight, but our time was. So we looked for the pieces we needed in furniture stores rather than at garage sales.

One Saturday our whole family was out together on a home-remodeling excursion. That's a nice way of saying we were dragging our poor kids to Lowe's for the ninety-third time to buy material for our remodeling project. We were all tired and wearing clothes that looked like they weren't good enough for a garage sale.

So there we were in all our fine glory. We'd purchased what we needed at Lowe's and proceeded to enter an upscale furniture store. And wouldn't you know it...we ran into a saleswoman who must have been the long-lost twin sister of that garage-sale man from all those years ago. Her ego was the size of South Dakota. She treated us like she thought we didn't have two pennies to rub together, and she really didn't have the time of day to deal with people of our class who had no business in that furniture store anyway. Daniel and I shared a silent communication of raised brows and a sour expression and took ourselves, our kids, and our money out of that store. We have no plans of ever returning.

When a person has a pride problem, the lofty attitude is usually the result of an *over-inflated ego*. Interestingly enough, the word "ego" was coined by Freud in the nineteenth century from the Latin word which means "I." When Austen wrote *Pride and Prejudice* in the late eighteenth century, she had never heard the word "ego" in terms of psychological behavior. However, she does a phenomenal job of modeling its existence in Darcy.

Even though I believe a streak of shyness plays a role in some of Darcy's actions (such as choosing not to dance with Elizabeth), he also exhibits many traits of being "blessed" with a swollen ego. And there isn't enough aspirin on the planet to reduce the swelling. Jane Austen's prescription for him is a sassy, outspoken female who isn't afraid to pare him down.

By the time Elizabeth Bennet gets through with Darcy, he screams "Uncle!" and winds up saying:

> *I have been a selfish being all my life, in practice, though not in principle. As a child, I was taught what was right; but I was not taught to correct my temper. I was given good principles, but left to follow them in pride and conceit. Unfortunately, an only son (for many years an only child), I was spoiled by my parents, who, though good themselves...allowed, encouraged, almost taught me to be selfish and overbearing—to care for none beyond my own family circle, to think meanly of all the rest of the world, to wish at least to think meanly of their sense and worth compared with my own. Such I was, from eight to eight-and-twenty; and such I might still have been but for you, dearest, loveliest Elizabeth! What do I not owe you? You taught me a lesson, hard indeed at first, but most advantageous. By you I was properly humbled. I came to you without a doubt of my reception. You showed me how insufficient were all my pretensions to please a woman worthy of being pleased.*[4]

Darcy is referencing Elizabeth's rejection of his proposal. When she gets through verbally thrashing him, he hits the door. According to Josh Billings, "One of the best temporary cures for pride and affection is seasickness; a man who wants to vomit never puts on airs." I think we could safely say that Darcy reels when Elizabeth tells him he's a jerk, but his sickness is more from love than the sea.

Dale Carnegie stated, "When dealing with people, remember you are not dealing with creatures of logic, but with creatures of emotion, creatures bristling with prejudice, and motivated by pride and vanity." Jane Austen's characters are so real that we often find ourselves saying, "I know someone exactly like that." Darcy and Elizabeth jump off the page because Austen creates multidimensional people who have positive attributes as well as blatant flaws. While Darcy strongly manifests a lofty attitude and an over-inflated ego, Elizabeth is guilty of *certainty of being right*, which can also be called closed-mindedness. Granted, Darcy comes across as having a certainty of being right during his proposal to Elizabeth. However, Elizabeth more consistently manifests this flaw throughout the book in many situations, including the situation with Wickham.

When Darcy proposes to Elizabeth, she has already embraced Mr. Wickham's lie about how Darcy has done him wrong. Because Darcy came across so arrogantly, Elizabeth had already been nursing a strong prejudice against him. She readily accepts Wickham's side of the story as the gospel. She is so certain of being right that she even brings up the Wickham saga in the wake of Darcy's proposal. She makes it remarkably clear that she has already tried and sentenced Darcy of the grossest of crimes against Wickham. And she is so certain she is so right that she blasts him with her opinion without any thought that there might be another side of the story.

Darcy is not willing to be verbally shot at without sharing *his* side of the story and showing Elizabeth that she's not as right as she thinks she is. He writes her a long letter detailing the true events of the Wickham story—that he is a philanderer who tried to seduce Darcy's younger sister into marrying him because of her large fortune.

"Prejudice is being down on something you're not up on," someone once said. Even though Elizabeth starts Darcy's letter with her prejudices intact, by the time she's read and reread it, she realizes she wasn't up on all the facts: "She grew absolutely ashamed of herself. Of neither Darcy nor Wickham could she think without feeling that she had been blind, partial, prejudiced, absurd."[5] And by the time her mind has been fully opened to the truth, she is realizing she has been as vain as she accused Darcy of being.

At this point Darcy and Elizabeth are like iron sharpening iron. They each have taken the other down a notch or two, and they each needed it. Darcy, certain that no woman in her right mind would reject a proposal from a man of his position and wealth, finds out that Elizabeth isn't interested. He's astounded that Elizabeth wouldn't jump at the chance of wealth, considering the fact that she is of low fortune and cannot inherit one splinter of her father's estate due to the gender-biased inheritance laws. What Elizabeth learns is that she isn't as right as she always thinks she is; that she, too, is guilty of the pride Darcy exhibits.

Many of us might find ourselves in this very position if we aren't careful. Too many times we criticize people for the very weaknesses we manifest ourselves. Honestly, one of my big temptations is to judge people who manifest gender, racial, and monetary prejudices. I believe such temptation is linked to the reason for Christ saying, "Do not judge, or you too will be judged. For in the same way you judge others, you will be judged, and with the measure you use, it will be measured to you" (Matthew 7:1-2). Too many times the judging we are doing is a manifestation of the same issue in ourselves. Furthermore, when we heap judgment upon others, too often they shove the same amount of judgment right back at us—like Darcy and Elizabeth do to each other. And then we really do reap what we have sown.

> *A great many people think they are thinking when they*
> *are merely rearranging their prejudices.*
> ~ WILLIAM JAMES ~

---

1. Jane Austen, *Pride and Prejudice*, The Complete Novels of Jane Austen, vol. I (New York: The Modern Library, 1992), p. 408.
2. Ibid., pp. 409, 411.
3. Ibid., p. 278.
4. Ibid., p. 537.
5. Ibid., p. 421.

Love is not rude...

~ 6 ~

Emma Woodhouse and
the Social Policeman

In everything, do to others what you would have them do to you.
~ Matthew 7:12 ~

Traveling and speaking can be a great adventure. Our family has seen most of the United States and many national parks during our travels. We've met people from all over the place and have made numerous friends—some that will last a lifetime. We've shared a lot of laughs and many memories that we'll celebrate for years.

One memory creator occurred just the other night during a trip to Atlanta, Georgia. We were getting ready for bed in our hotel room and were about to turn out the lights. I wanted to tell my son to give me a goodnight kiss. But instead I said, "Come, give Mama a good-night *hiss*." We laughed out loud. He came across the room, and we spontaneously put our faces within inches of each other and hissed. Several times since then, we've exchanged good-night hisses in place of good-night kisses. My son is 11 and thinks this is the most hilarious thing in the world.

Even though traveling and speaking have their advantages, the life also has a downside. Frankly, by the time we get home we're usually so exhausted we're too tired to hiss or kiss. Furthermore, nearly every time we go somewhere my husband and I both wonder who's going to be rude this time. It almost never fails. Someone usually makes certain we get a double helping of rude before the trip is over. Sometimes it's the conference center director or the hotel manager or even a mean-spirited conference attendee.

Daniel and I never cease to be amazed at the people who are royally rude and never apologize. All of us have moments when we blow it, and when we do, we should apologize to the affected parties. Through the years we've learned to hold our tongues and smile and tell ourselves we won't have to deal with the rude one for long.

Just as we all have flaws, so do Jane Austen's characters. Emma Woodhouse has a problem with being rude. She is a delightfully imperfect heroine, and most Austen fans love her. She's nosy, strong-willed, controlling, and a little too sassy for her own good. I've dubbed her the "Queen of Sass."

She also has the unfortunate fate of being over-indulged by a governess who is more like an elder sister than a mother figure. Emma's mother died young, and Emma's father joins in the doting that turns Emma into the young lady who bursts upon the pages of the novel named after her.

Her male counterpart, George Knightley, believes it's his duty to correct Emma's faults. He spends many years as an elder brother figure who swiftly challenges her about her shortcomings as soon as she trots them out for the world to see. Despite himself and Emma's failures, Knightley winds up falling in love with her...as does the reader.

Think of an over-eager St. Bernard who's only nine months old. Most breeds of large dogs don't realize how big they really are when they're half-grown puppies. In their hearts they're still babies despite the fact that their bodies are huge. Such canines will usually knock you flat and lick your whole face. By the time it's over, you're a slobbered-up mess, but you've got to laugh because the dog is just so adorable.

So it goes with Emma. Even though she has obvious faults and she sometimes doesn't realize her own power, she's still so witty and charming you've got to adore her. Poor Knightley doesn't stand a chance. He falls and falls hard.

One of Emma's flaws is that she is prone to insulting people, which is rude. Her most famous and most unfortunate insult is against Miss Bates, her lifelong friend:

> *"Ladies and gentlemen," [Frank Churchill declared], "I am ordered by Miss Woodhouse to say that she waives her right of knowing exactly what you may all be thinking of, and only...demands from each of you, either one thing very clever, be*

> *it prose or verse, original or repeated; or two things moderately clever; or three things very dull indeed; and she engages to laugh heartily at them all."*
>
> *"Oh! very well," exclaimed Miss Bates; "then I need not be uneasy. 'Three things very dull indeed.' That will just do for me, you know. I shall be sure to say three dull things as soon as ever I open my mouth, shan't I?" (looking round with the most good-humoured dependence on everybody's assent). "Do not you all think I shall?"*
>
> *Emma could not resist.*
>
> *"Ah! ma'am, but there may be a difficulty. Pardon me, but you will be limited as to number—only three at once."*[1]

As a woman with a sharp mind, Emma sometimes is too quick to speak. Her insult to Miss Bates is blatant in-your-face rudeness. However, she also manifests subtle rudeness, and behind-your-back rudeness. Unfortunately we all have been guilty of rudeness—or been on the receiving end.

> *The slight that can be conveyed in a glance, in a gracious smile, in a wave of the hand, is often the ne plus ultra of art. What insult is so keen or so keenly felt, as the polite insult which it is impossible to resent.*
>
> ~ JULIA KAVANAGH ~

In-Your-Face Rudeness

How many times have most of us opened our mouths and

said things we wished we could take back? I often jokingly say I'm the "Mouth of the South." Once my sister-in-law gave me a plaque that read, "Be sure brain is engaged before putting mouth into gear." The plaque was replete with a picture of a man with a wide-open mouth the size of the Grand Canyon.

My big crime is that sometimes I say things that might be interpreted as rude when my intent really is pure. As I mature, I'm trying to filter what I say by asking myself, "Will this be something that will haunt me later?"

Even though Emma's faults blend together to enhance her charm, when she insults Miss Bates she comes across as anything but endearing. She should have asked herself the above question before she cut down Miss Bates. The poor lady's flaky nature would probably try the nerves of a saint; however, she's a harmless woman who's due Emma's respect from the very fact that she's been Emma's lifelong friend and devotee. However, Emma's tongue gets the best of her when she essentially tells Miss Bates she's as dull as a used-up dust rag.

Instead of getting angry and denying that she's got a problem, Miss Bates is genuinely hurt. Furthermore, she embraces the insult as truth and believes she must have been really bad for Emma to say something so pointed. Initially Emma shows no regrets for hurling the verbal dart at her friend and neighbor. But that's before Emma's "social policeman" wastes no time and confronts her, awakening her conscience. George Knightley tells Emma she messed up big. By the time Knightley gets through,

Emma is a remorseful shell of her former self…and well she should be.

> *Never had she felt so agitated, mortified, grieved, at any circumstance in her life. She was most forcibly struck. The truth of his representation there was no denying. She felt it at her heart. How could she have been so brutal, so cruel to Miss Bates! How could she have exposed herself to such ill opinion in any one she valued!…She never had been so depressed…and Emma felt the tears running down her cheeks almost all the way home, without being at any trouble to check them, extraordinary as they were.*[2]

Whether we're rude on purpose, as is Emma, or viewed as rude because of our lack of verbal prudence, we are well served to learn from the situation. Love is not rude. And if someone has been hurt, whether we meant to harm him or her or not, we are responsible before God for showing love and building bridges to repair relationships.

But remember, there are some people who are so insecure, they accuse others of rudeness even if none has transpired. While the Lord does expect us to make restitution when we're wrong, He never requires us to take responsibility for someone else's sin or emotional baggage. If you're finding yourself always apologizing to someone who falsely accuses you of insulting them, it might be a good idea to get some space on that relationship. Otherwise, it might become a sick, festering sore in your life that drags you down and keeps you down.

Subtle Rudeness

I'll never forget a boy named Davie in my first-grade class. Davie was a chubby kid who hovered over his plate at lunch time and inhaled his food. Looking back, I believe Davie manifested some symptoms of a neurological eating compulsion that can plague people from birth. I also have a hunch that Davie's stomach never was able to communicate a "you're full" message to his brain due to miswiring between the stomach and brain. All that is to say that I don't believe Davie could help the way he ate. And even if his parents were coaching him about table manners, he was probably too young for a full correction.

One day my first-grade teacher came by our table while Davie was eating. With a sarcastic smile she made a "cut you to the heart" comment about Davie's eating and weight in a subtly soft voice. Even though I can't remember exactly what she said, I'll never forget Davie's expression. With his face hovering over his food, a spoon touching his lips, he gazed up at the teacher with a look in his eyes that hurts me to this day. The look said, "I'm not too young to understand what you meant. I don't deserve what you said. It hurts. And I know there's not a thing in the world I can do about it."

Really, just thinking about this angers me, even after 35 years. I don't understand why some people purposefully make critical and hateful comments to anyone, let alone children. Don't they understand they're probably scarring them for life?

Subtle rudeness, whether directed at children or adults, can be more harmful than in-your-face rudeness. Some people have the ability to charmingly deliver a rude barb that's only felt by the victim; the rest of the room misses the whole thing. Then there's the short-lived glare, the cold-shoulder treatment, and the snooty attitudes. While nothing rude is necessarily said, the message is clear and communicated loudly. This kind of subtlety takes a significant level of determined skill that can be downright cold-blooded and mean-spirited.

Emma practices her ability to let someone know she's not enamored with them when she encounters Augusta Elton. But Emma shows remarkable constraint to keep her dislike subtly detectable in the face of Augusta's obnoxiousness.

Another kind of subtle rudeness involves such things as a visit never paid, a responsibility never taken. Often this rudeness hurts as much as the blatant insult because it's a silent slap in the face or a quiet "you don't matter." Emma succumbs to this level of rudeness in her dealings with Miss Bates and her mother. Even though Emma understands that she should visit the ladies more and is expected to visit them more, she refuses because she just doesn't want to:

> *She had had many a hint from Mr. Knightley, and some from her own heart, as to her deficiency, but none were equal to counteract the persuasion of its being very disagreeable—a waste of time—tiresome women—and all the horror of being in danger of falling in with the second rate and third rate of Highbury, who were calling on them for ever, and therefore she seldom went near them.*[3]

A dash of snobbery rounds off rudeness nicely, don't you think?

Once George Knightley pulls his "social policeman" act again, Emma is not only driven to tears, but also to a repentance so thorough that the reader has trouble even remembering that "dear, sweet Emma" ever struggled with a haughty spirit or any level of rudeness: "In the warmth of true contrition she would call upon [Miss Bates] the very next morning, and it should be the beginning, on her side, of a regular, equal, kindly intercourse."[4]

Sometimes love requires us to do things we'd really rather not do—such as visit needy people because we value their emotions and welfare more than we value our own mental comfort. I'm not suggesting that we place ourselves in abusive situations or anything unhealthy. Nevertheless, there's a world full of hurting people out there who might be a little flaky, but they need friends anyway.

Some of them might even be relatives. I never cease to be amazed at the number of parents or siblings and sons or daughters who neglect the care of their close relatives simply because they don't have time or, like Emma with Miss Bates, they just don't want to go visit them no matter how much they are needed. So they ignore the relative in need and never consider that it's a form of rudeness. Such abandonment can go beyond rudeness and be heartbreaking for the neglected relative or neighbor.

Behind-Your-Back Rudeness

As noted in Matthew 7:12, Jesus states the Golden Rule:

"In everything, do to others what you would have them do to you, for this sums up the Law and the Prophets." This verse applies to *every* relationship we have and every moment of our lives. If everyone lived out this one verse, all crime worldwide would end. It would revolutionize relationships. It would annihilate all class-conscious snobbery, gender and racial prejudices, child abuse, and rudeness. And that's just for starters.

Even though the world suffers because of the lack of applying the Golden Rule, I believe one of the prominent places this verse is least applied is when we speak ill of others when they aren't around. Good people can be so brutal with behind-the-back slams. I've repeatedly listened to people be horribly critical of someone, but they're *so* nice to that person when he or she is present. Like Emma, we've probably all been guilty of similar behavior at one time or another and had to repent.

Early in the novel, Emma decides Harriet Smith should not marry Mr. Martin because he's not the "quality" of man she deserves. Emma has never even *met* Mr. Martin; nevertheless, she sets out to discredit him to Harriet based on the fact that he comes from the working class. In modern terms, the guy is from the wrong side of the tracks, and as far as Emma is concerned there's nothing going to bump him to the right side.

When Emma does meet Robert Martin, she says, "He is plain, undoubtedly; remarkably plain; but that is nothing compared with his entire want of gentility. I had no right to expect much, and I did not expect much; but I had no idea that he could be so very clownish, so totally without air. I had imagined him,

I confess, a degree or two nearer gentility."[5] Emma is slamming a man she has never had one conversation with. In reality, he's a hard worker, a good catch, and very much in love with Harriet. A woman of questionable birth, Harriet could do much worse in an offer of marriage. But when Robert Martin proposes, Emma manipulates Harriet into rejecting him.

Knightley, a champion of Mr. Martin, is furious. When Emma explains that she doesn't believe Martin is Harriet's equal, Knightley tells her she's crazy. As the book progresses, the reader clearly sees that Knightley is right about Mr. Martin and Emma is wrong.

In the same conversation, Knightley also tells her, "Emma, your infatuation about that girl blinds you."[6] Essentially, Emma is just as blind about Harriet Smith and all the matchmaking plans she has for her as Elizabeth Bennet from *Pride and Prejudice* is blind about Darcy's good qualities. Yet Emma remains determined she is irrevocably right and continues in her insulting views of Robert Martin.

Only at the book's ending, after she's played havoc with Harriet Smith's love life, and Harriet decides she's in love with George Knightley, does Emma have a change of heart. Just as she repents of her ill treatment of Miss Bates, so Emma repents of all her insults against Robert Martin and her botched matchmaking schemes. She wallows in a pool of regret as she imagines that Knightley returns Harriet's love and the two will marry.

Any time we stoop to any form of insult or manipulation, we usually wind up exactly where Emma Woodhouse does:

remorseful. Conversely, when we truly live the Golden Rule, it requires that we set aside our own interests and put ourselves in the place of others. In order to do this, we must totally remove ourselves from our ego-centric position and see things from the other person's viewpoint. This changes everything because it detaches us from selfish plans or desires that we might hold dear. Once separated, we have a greater chance of seeing the person we're tempted to insult as God sees him or her, and thus have a greater chance of extending grace to the person as God extends to us.

> *Most rude behavior is based on disrespect.*
> *When we truly respect others, we leave insults*
> *behind and treat people of all races, gender,*
> *and social standing with dignity.*

---

1. Jane Austen, *Emma*, The Complete Novels of Jane Austen, vol. II (New York: The Modern Library, 1992), pp. 269-70.

2. Ibid., p. 274.

3. Ibid., p. 111.

4. Ibid., p. 275.

5. Ibid., p. 23.

6. Ibid., p. 44.

Love is not self-seeking...

Lydia Bennet and the Wickham Snake

*Now the serpent was more crafty than any of the wild
animals the LORD God had made.*
~ GENESIS 3:1 ~

I recently watched a news documentary about a 14-year-old Australian girl, Tammy, who came up missing. Tammy's parents and the local authorities launched an all-out task force to find the girl but found nothing. About three years after she disappeared, the family finally accepted the fact that the girl was dead, most likely murdered, and held a memorial service for her. They grieved her loss as if she were in a casket before their eyes. Friends and family turned out; the media covered the event.

Finally a serial killer confessed to several gruesome murders and eventually admitted to killing Tammy as well. He told the authorities where he killed three victims, and they found the remains. The serial killer also said he killed Tammy near an abandoned house in the country and that he buried her beneath a mango tree. The authorities scoured the area but found no evidence of the girl's remains. However, since the serial killer had confessed to the other murders and they found the other victims' remains, they believed the killer had indeed killed Tammy.

The serial killer was on trial for the murder of four women, including Tammy. Tammy's father was at the trial, making sure the killer would face the family of one of his victims. Then the authorities received an unexpected tip. A girl meeting Tammy's description was seen in the area. Authorities responded to the tip and found Tammy alive and well within a mile of her mother's home.

She'd run away with an older man and lived with him in his apartment for four years. At night, she'd sometimes go to the beach. In the daytime, she stayed out of sight. Any time visitors came into the apartment, she'd hide in a closet until they left. When the police discovered her, she was in the closet hiding from them.

All those years she had watched the media and known she was presumed dead by her family. She'd witnessed their grieving and had seen the information in the newspaper. She even knew the serial killer was on trial for her murder, but she never came forward. She remained incognito and in the relationship with the man she'd run off with.

With the serial killer's trial in full swing, she was subpoenaed to court to state that she was not dead so the serial killer could not be tried for her murder.

Meanwhile her parents, who were divorced, had different reactions to her appearance. Her father was so thrilled to see her he didn't care what she'd put him through. Her mother stated that she was enraged and wanted to slap Tammy. However, after the anger wore off the mother was just thankful Tammy was alive. Presently Tammy's father is estranged from her; her mother has a relationship with her but says she doesn't trust her. I wonder why.

Once Tammy's story was known, she was a bigger news item than ever. But she refused to be interviewed by anyone unless they paid her. Finally someone paid her a hundred grand for an interview. Tammy got an agent and began to make money on the horrible crime she'd committed against her family.

The man she was living with wound up going to prison for lying to the police. Presently, new charges have been pressed against both of them. In the end, they both may have to pay back the money the police department spent trying to find Tammy.

When I first heard the story, my reaction was "that girl should have to repay every penny she cost the community in their search for her." Frankly, I'm astounded that someone could sit and watch her parents and a whole community grieve her death and search for her body while remaining in hiding. Tammy is either mentally unbalanced or unbelievably cold-hearted. When asked if her lover had coerced her into staying in hiding, she coolly responded that she had chosen to hide on her own. Logic insists that Tammy's boyfriend played a role in her choices and should bear at least part of the responsibility

I lean toward thinking both Tammy and her boyfriend are cold-hearted and selfish. If the girl is levelheaded enough to get an agent and charge money for interviews, then she most likely has all—or most—of her mental faculties. And her boyfriend did lie to authorities in the face of knowing what havoc Tammy's disappearance was playing with her family and the community.

Have you ever met any people like Tammy and her lover? I have. There's even a word for them: narcissistic—named after a character in Greek mythology, Narcissus, who loved nothing more than looking at his own reflection. These people are so self-absorbed they wouldn't feel an ounce of remorse if they maimed someone for life, just as long as they got what they wanted. According to Charles H. Parkhurst, "The man who lives by himself and for himself is likely to be corrupted by the company he keeps." Interestingly enough, this corruption feeds upon itself, breeds more corruption, and sucks the narcissist's soul into a never-ending spiral of selfishness.

While most decent people know these types exist and don't want them or their children to be duped by them, the world abounds with them. Nations are full of stories of people and families who are severely wounded by such characters. That's because they aren't easily spotted. They are often very good at hiding their self-seeking tendencies behind a beguiling veil. They don't boast; they charm. They don't repel; they win friends. They're as subtle and wicked as the cunning serpent in the Garden of Eden. They're venomous snakes awaiting the right moment to strike and swallow the latest prey.

In many of Jane Austen's novels there's a subplot similar to the Australian saga. A self-seeking person runs off with another character. Often the plot involves a fickle, immature young woman who lets her emotions rule and escapes with some man of ill repute—and not for a nice little poetry reading, either. *Pride and Prejudice* is no exception. This is hot stuff for 1797, but these situations did happen even then. Despite our assumptions that the twentieth and twenty-first centuries are more wicked than previous ages, many eras in history oozed blatant immorality that would reap a blush or two today. Some of Austen's contemporary observations included young chicks and silver-tongued devils who were a little too wild and willing for their own good.

Lydia Bennet is such a young chick, and Wickham's tongue couldn't be more silver if he had it plated in sterling. The two of them are more interested in having a good time than whether anyone is hurt by their behavior. To say Lydia's family is scandalized by her affair is an understatement. In that culture when a daughter blatantly slept with a man out of wedlock, the whole family was tarnished, which could result in social death.

But neither Lydia nor Wickham cared. Lydia, a high-spirited 15-year-old, is too immature and self-absorbed to worry about how her choices will scar her family. And I don't think Wickham could care about anyone but himself even if he tried. The letter from Mr. Gardiner to Mr. Bennet confirms that, like Tammy, both Wickham and Lydia are interested only in gratifying their desires without considering the pain to their families:

> *My Dear Brother…At last I am able to send you some tidings of my niece, and such as, upon the whole, I hope will give you satisfaction. Soon after you left me on Saturday, I was fortunate enough to find out in what part of London they were…I have seen them both. They are not married, nor can I find there was any intention of being so; but if you are willing to perform the engagements which I have ventured to make on your side, I hope it will not be long before they are.*[1]

By the time Wickham and Lydia run off together, Wickham has already tried to dupe Darcy's sister into marrying him. His driving passion is her large fortune and has nothing to do with his feelings for her. He's got to be every woman's dream man.

Jane Austen obviously knew this type well when she crafted Wickham. While Lydia selfishly lives for the moment, Wickham charms with a motive. He plots. He conquers his prey and tries to take what he wants. With Darcy's sister, it's her money; with Lydia, it's her virginity. Wickham wins the title of "The Snake."

Serpents like Wickham are all too common. Furthermore, they're as good at duping as they are at hiding their sins. Wickham certainly fools Elizabeth into believing he's a sad, sorry victim of mean ol' Darcy's evil schemes. And Elizabeth Bennet is no dummy by any means. Elizabeth's believing Wickham also fuels her initial disdain for Darcy. Nevertheless, Wickham is still very convincing, Darcy dislike or no.

The last thing any of us wants is to be struck by a snake. Nevertheless, if we're not careful, it might be our families who are crushed by the likes of a Wickham. Wickham-snakes slither through every town and culture. They can be male or female and of any race. Unfortunately, they're even in churches…sometimes on the pew…sometimes in the pulpit. If you want to guard yourself and your family from such rascals, you must understand the warning signs.

> *That man who lives for self alone, lives*
> *for the meanest mortal known.*
> ~ JOAQUIN MILLER ~

Warning Sign #1: Rascals are highly appealing

"Love is not self-seeking." Selfishness is the opposite of love. When you think of others before yourself, you are living love. People who plot to be self-seeking are the most loveless of all. They aren't merely living for themselves by natural default, they slyly conspire to take what others have for their own selfish gain.

Wickham-snakes purposefully use their charm for selfish purposes. These people are glib-tongued scoundrels who come prepared to woo with their lies in one hand and their compliments in the other. On top of that, they're usually very well groomed and appear decent. They might not necessarily be as classically handsome as Wickham, but they will have the appearance of being a person of high morals, a person you should believe in.

When Wickham arrives on the scene in *Pride and Prejudice*, he makes an impressive appearance. He's good-looking, has great manners, is charming, is a great conversationalist, and on top of that, he's a soldier. Elizabeth and everyone else think, "Wow!"

The next time Wickham shows up, he attends a gathering at the Philips'. Wickham focuses upon Elizabeth and charms her into a purring fit. By the time Wickham gets through talking with Elizabeth, "his manners recommended him to everybody. Whatever he said, was said well; and whatever he did, done gracefully. Elizabeth went away with her head full of him. She could think of nothing but of Mr. Wickham, and of what he had told her, all the way home."[2]

Wickham is like a fisherman throwing a hook laced with tantalizing bait to a prime perch. Elizabeth is his fish of choice. And she readily swallows the succulent lies because the person delivering them is so irrevocably charming and well-groomed she can't do anything but accept his honesty. Wickham has her hooked. She's all his.

So it goes with any Wickham-snake. These people are usually so smooth they could convince the world of bold-faced lies and never blink. They're also not always males. I've seen a prime young man duped by this type, only to discover *after* the marriage that his wife is a conniving witch. Since the young man is too honorable to ditch his witchy wife, he's sentenced to a life of misery. I've watched young ladies lured into illicit affairs by men who promised undying love, as is Lydia Bennet. Then I've seen whole congregations fooled into believing the pastor or deaconess is the "real deal," and they're so blind they wind up agreeing to even pay the leader's way out of a felony...and all because the person is so convincing that good-hearted people are thoroughly hoodwinked. If the Wickham-snake also has the fortune of being classically handsome or beautiful, that adds amps to their power.

Not every good-looking, well-groomed, polite person is a Wickham-snake. And I don't recommend that anyone runs scared every time he or she meets this type. As a matter of fact, most people I know who are attractive, well-groomed, and polite *aren't* Wickham-snakes. However, Wickham-snakes almost always use their positive attributes as tools of manipulation. As did the serpent in the Garden of Eden, they purposefully project the best light possible upon themselves to better connive and take advantage.

Warning Sign #2: Rascals present themselves as victims

When I wrote *First Impressions*, based on *Pride and Prejudice*, I created a modern version of Wickham in Rick Wallace. Like Wickham, Rick comes onto the scene with a sob story about how Dave Davidson (my Darcy) does him wrong. Rick is Dave's foster cousin. According to Rick, Dave is jealous because their grandfather loved Rick, a foster grandson, as much as he loved his biological grandchildren. So Dave allegedly blackballs him at the seminaries Rick plans to apply to. No school will admit him as a student; therefore, he can't pursue the ministry as he plans. Eddi Boswick (my Elizabeth Bennet) believes Rick.

But as in *Pride and Prejudice*, there's another side to the story.

As Darcy writes Elizabeth with a full explanation, so Dave writes Eddi:

> *The end of my senior year of high school, I learned that Rick had been playing around with drugs and alcohol…He had just made a profession of faith at church and was saying he thought he should go into the ministry. But the negative reports came more and more often until finally I couldn't ignore them.*
>
> *One night, the year after I graduated from high school…I decided to follow [Rick]. What I witnessed was Rick buying marijuana and then picking up a woman who was much older and far from being a lady.*
>
> *Strangely, he had just begun to send out applications to seminary and was saying God had called him to be a pastor. See, our grandfather had died and left money for Rick to attend seminary. I guess Rick figured it was his free ticket to college, I don't know. Anyway, when I found out about Rick's true character, I did the only thing I knew to do. I told my father, who did the only thing he knew to do. He made the seminaries Rick had applied to aware of the issues. Needless to say, Rick wasn't able to get into the seminaries, and I believe the ministry at large was saved a scandal.[3]*

Most Wickham-snakes arrive on the scene with a horrible story about how they were traumatized by some mean ol' person who misused them. Sometimes that person is in the area; sometimes he isn't. But the scenario is usually the same:

The Wickham-snake presents him- or herself as the undeserving recipient of someone's heartless actions.

As with the original Wickham and my version of him, many times the "meanie" they say has hurt them is wealthy or socially prominent. That's because people just love to think ill of the wealthy or well-known. This is probably rooted in deep-seated envy. When someone *wants* to be rich or renowned but isn't, then that person will resent those who are. They mask their envy in dislike and are thrilled when they hear a story that validates their disdain.

In *Pride and Prejudice*, Elizabeth Bennet doesn't like Darcy because she views him as an arrogant jerk. Jane Austen doesn't indicate that envy plays a role in Elizabeth's scorn. After all, Darcy *does* insult her early in the book when he says she's not pretty enough for him to dance with. That's enough to make any woman in any century sprout horns and blow red smoke out of her ears *and* nose. So Elizabeth already can't stand the sight of Darcy. When Wickham comes out with his sob story, Elizabeth grabs it and hangs on to it because the scenario gives her even more reason to validate her near-hatred.

True to his snake nature, Wickham weaves a saga that's nothing more than a rotten lie. According to him, Darcy refuses to give him the clergy living Darcy Sr. promised him before he died. In modern terms, Wickham claims he's supposed to be the local preacher in Darcy's neighborhood and is close to being ordained. But when Darcy's father dies, Darcy takes measures to stop Wickham's ordination and his livelihood...and all allegedly because Darcy is jealous because his father views Wickham as a favorite. Elizabeth, already "out of love" with Darcy, embraces the story and is thrilled to hear any juicy piece of information that will reinforce her mounting prejudices.

"This is quite shocking," [Elizabeth says.] "He deserves to be publicly disgraced."[4] Ironically, the person who deserves to be publicly disgraced is Wickham. But Elizabeth refuses to even consider there might be another side to the story.

And so it goes with many Wickham-snake victims. Too many times people are too eager to hear one side of a story and not investigate the story's authenticity. I once heard that in any conflict there are three sides: your side, their side, and the right side. While I do believe this is often true, I also know there are situations like the Wickham/Darcy scenario where a scoundrel brutally tries to take advantage of people.

Through the years I've saved myself some grief and the tragedy of being duped by understanding that any time someone claims to have been victimized, there is often more to the story than they are telling. Sometimes I investigate; other times I wait for the other half of the story to float to me. Occasionally I will learn that the person really was fully victimized. It does happen. But more often than not, the other side of the story puts everything in a different light.

Warning Sign #3: Rascals always leave clues

I live in east Texas, and in my part of the country tornadoes abound. While tornadoes sometimes take residents by surprise, we've learned to watch the clouds and often can tell the difference between a tornado-producing storm and one that's merely a good rainstorm. This ability comes in handy when we're traveling. We often have to drive through storms. My 11-year-old son is as terrified of and fascinated with tornadoes as I was at his age. Any time we drive through a rain, Brett gets nervous and asks, "Mama, is this tornado weather?" More likely than not, I'll say, "No. It's just a good rain."

However, this past spring we were driving near Hot Springs, Arkansas, and ran into some weather that was not just a rain. This storm was replete with large hail; horrible lightning; black, swirling clouds; blinding rain; and wind so strong the trees were bending toward the earth. Leaves and pine needles hit the windshield as violently as the rain.

When my son worriedly asked if this was tornado weather, I had to be honest. "Yes. This is tornado weather. Start praying now!"

Even my husband, who's not scared of the weather, had a grim look on his face. I relived a scene from 12 years ago when I was expecting Brett. I drove through identical weather while the Emergency Broadcast System was sending out a warning over the radio to take cover if you were exactly where I was because there was a tornado on the ground. It wouldn't have surprised me in either situation to see a funnel pass in front of the vehicle. Why? Because I know what clues to watch for when a tornado is nearby: blinding rain, hail, high winds, and if there are trees, leaves flying everywhere.

Wickham-snakes can be just as destructive as tornadoes. Any time a Wickham-snake is on the scene, he (or she) inevitably leaves clues that reveal his destructive nature. The problem lies with the people being conned. Like Elizabeth Bennet, many times the victims are so hooked, they refuse to acknowledge the clues, let alone investigate them. If Elizabeth had seriously looked into Wickham's whopper, she'd have saved herself the embarrassment of having to admit she was wrong about Darcy.

The truth is, Darcy has to intervene to stop Wickham from taking advantage of his 15-year-old sister who has the equivalent of a million dollar fortune (in modern dollars). How *convenient* that Wickham "falls in love" with her! And yes, Darcy does prohibit Wickham from becoming a clergyman, but he does it as a decent man stopping a morally bankrupt con-artist from violating the ministry.

As for Elizabeth, she is given numerous hints at the Netherfield ball that Wickham's story is false, but she stubbornly refuses to believe them. Before the hints begin, Darcy asks Elizabeth to dance, and the invitation so addles her, she accepts. When Elizabeth frets to Charlotte Lucas about having to dance with Darcy, Charlotte encourages her with, "I dare say you might find him very agreeable." And Elizabeth comes out with a witty quote, "Heaven forbid! *That* would be the greatest misfortune of all! To find a man agreeable whom one is determined to hate! Do not wish me such an evil."[5]

With this mind-set, Elizabeth dismisses every clue to Wickham's true character that's flung at her feet. First she questions

Darcy about Wickham. Unfortunately, her attitude is not that of an open-minded investigator; rather, Elizabeth proves herself closed-minded, prejudiced, and against believing anything other than Wickham's side of the story. Darcy insinuates that there's more to Wickham's tale than she believes, but Elizabeth ignores this hint.

And she keeps on ignoring the truths that fall at her feet like succulent chocolates ready to be gobbled up. Instead, she kicks them out of her way and continues in her blind prejudices against Darcy. Miss Bingley informs Elizabeth that "Wickham has treated Mr. Darcy in a most infamous manner."[6] Then Elizabeth's sister, Jane, reports that Bingley himself supports Darcy's innocence and believes that "Wickham is by no means a respectable young man."[7] By this point even Jane, who never wants to believe anything ill of anyone, suspects that Wickham has a dark side. But Elizabeth, so wrapped up in her determination to hate Darcy and believe Wickham, doesn't even recognize this as a clue.

Too many times this scenario is played out in real life. I have known of numerous tragic situations, including child molestation, that could have been avoided by someone merely making a few phone calls to investigate a Wickham-snake's past. But people tend to decide to believe what they want about a particular person and refuse to listen to the internal doubts often placed there by God or to the external clues sometimes left by the snake and sometimes dropped by others.

While Elizabeth's story is carefully crafted by Jane Austen, our lives are crafted by God. And in the real world, God often places very clear clues in our paths that will implicate the Wickham-snakes in our midst. Many times, the snakes leave clues themselves. But too often, we can be like Elizabeth, determined not to believe the clues even if they bite us on the nose.

> *When we abhor the very thought of making choices that will hurt others, we have learned to love others as much as ourselves.*

---

1. Jane Austen, *Pride and Prejudice*, The Complete Novels of Jane Austen, vol. I (New York: The Modern Library, 1992), p. 487.

2. Ibid., p. 333.

3. Debra White Smith, *First Impressions* (Eugene, OR: Harvest House Publishers, 2004), pp. 242-43.

4. Austen, *Pride and Prejudice*, p. 329.

5. Ibid., p. 337.

6. Ibid., p. 340.

7. Ibid., p. 341.

Love is not easily angered…

~ 8 ~

Elinor Dashwood and the Wasp's Nest

The intoxication of anger, like that of the grape, shows us to others, but hides us from ourselves. We injure our own cause in the opinion of the world when we too passionately defend it.

~ CHARLES CALEB COLTON ~

Craig had a very difficult father. His father, Harry, was controlling, nosy, and somewhat neurotic. Harry never stopped talking. When he was alone, he even talked nonstop to himself. Harry also thrived on conflict. He continually kept the family stirred up by misstating what one of his adult children had said about the other. By the time Harry got through twisting the story, it was completely different from what was intended, and his children became angry with each other.

His father's neurotic talking drove Craig nuts. There was never a time that he didn't blow up in an angry explosion of verbiage when he was with his dad. As the years stretched on,

Craig and Harry lived in a perpetual state of conflict. That was the total nature of their relationship.

While Craig loved his father, he possessed no tools to manage his anger when he was with his dad. Admittedly, some of that anger stemmed from childhood issues, including the fact that his mother abandoned the family and Harry was too heavy-handed when it came to discipline. But these issues aside, Harry was still a very difficult person to live with and to deal with.

Wouldn't it be wonderful if all family dynamics were like those on the *Andy Griffith Show*, *Leave It to Beaver*, and *The Cosby Show*? Unfortunately, in real life family dynamics can become a negative force rather than the positive support God intended.

Many families have one or two neurotic members. Like Harry these people can't help it if they're weird and paranoid and talk all the time. And some family groups are "blessed" with a few takers. These people don't know how to give. All they are good at is taking and complaining about those who give to them. There are also those like Craig who have anger problems and are apt to explode at any given moment. And, of course, there are the family members who are selfish, mean-spirited, and wouldn't bring you a cup of cold water if you were dying of thirst. Apparently Jane Austen knew a few of these. Fanny Dashwood, in *Sense and Sensibility*, perfectly fits this description:

> *No sooner was his father's funeral over, than Mrs. John [Fanny] Dashwood, without sending any notice of her intention to her mother-in-law, arrived with her child and their attendants. No one could dispute her right to come; the house*

was her husband's from the moment of his father's decease; but the indelicacy of her conduct was so much the greater, and to a woman in Mrs. Dashwood's situation, with only common feelings, must have been highly unpleasing…[and] was to her a source of immovable disgust. Mrs. John Dashwood had never been a favourite with any of her husband's family: but she had had not opportunity till the present, of showing them with how little attention to the comfort of other people she could act when occasion required it.

So acutely did Mrs. Dashwood feel this ungracious behaviour, and so earnestly did she despise her daughter-in-law for it, that, on the arrival of the latter, she would have quitted the house for ever, had not the entreaty of her eldest girl induced her first to reflect on the propriety of going, and her own tender love for all her three children determined her afterwards to stay, and for their sakes avoid a breach with their brother.

Elinor, this eldest daughter whose advice was so effectual, possessed a strength of understanding, and coolness of judgment, which qualified her, though only nineteen, to be the counselor of her mother, and enabled her frequently to counteract, to the advantage of them all, that eagerness of mind in Mrs. Dashwood which must generally have led to imprudence.[1]

Jane Austen had the amazing ability to clearly draw characters distinctively different from each other. In *Sense and Sensibility*, Austen presents a contrast in calm, resolute Elinor Dashwood and her flighty mother and sister. The difference in these women is like the difference between a trained German shepherd that sizes up every situation and a couple of over-strung poodles who can't control their energy.

At the ripe old age of 19, Elinor remains calm under most circumstances and even advises her mother how to behave in a high-stress situation. Fortunately, most families are blessed with a few levelheaded, self-controlled members who are not selfish takers, angry, neurotic, or complainers. In the Dashwood family, Elinor stands out as the "Most Sensible." Granted, Austen shows that Elinor is a little too logically cool while Marianne is too flighty. By the book's end, both sisters have gone through the Jane Austen School of Character Adjustment and been brought to a greater degree of balance: more sensibility for Elinor and more sense for Marianne. However, if I were to have to choose to err on one side or the other, I'd rather be a bit too logical and in control of my mind than too flighty and irresponsible. The logical one usually stays out of trouble and away from scandal.

So it goes for Elinor when her sister-in-law moves into the Dashwood estate with no thought for the feelings of her in-laws. The poor Dashwood women find themselves at the height of stress. As already mentioned, inheritance laws of that era stank. That's the problem Mrs. Henry Dashwood and her three daughters face in the opening pages of *Sense and Sensibility*.

Mr. Henry Dashwood has died. If *that's* not bad enough, his vast property, Norland estate, and the living that goes with it are left to his son, John Dashwood. John is the offspring of Henry's first marriage. Remember, no woman—not even a wife—was allowed to inherit property. Therefore, Mrs. Dashwood's stepson is now legally entitled to claim the estate along with his haughty-snob-of-a-wife, Fanny. Jane Austen describes her as "narrow-minded and selfish."[2] Other than these magnificent traits, she's a really nice person.

This fine specimen of a stepdaughter-in-law barely gives Henry Dashwood time to chill in his grave before she moves into Norland Park with her child and attendants and shoves "Mrs. Henry" and her daughters out of the way. They are "degraded to the condition of visitors" in their own home.[3] Now isn't that just peachy? On top of that, "Mrs. John" doesn't even have the decency to tell Mrs. Henry she's coming. She just shows up with the expectation that Mrs. Henry and her three daughters will move along now that their husband and father has died.

Mrs. Henry does what most of us would do in that situation: She nearly blows a gasket. But Elinor, the calm, collected one, talks her out of it. And Elinor does this sort of thing throughout the book. Just about the time her mother or sister or the reader is ready to snatch a character bald, Elinor comes along with her levelheaded reasoning and reminds everyone why it would be so much better to remain calm and not say or do something that will later be regretted.

Would that we all could be that way *all* the time. Unfortunately, most of us aren't. Too many times we find ourselves behaving like Craig and reacting on the spur of the moment by saying or doing things we'll later regret. I've found myself in this situation enough times to finally learn to hold my tongue until I and the situation have cooled. Well, most of the time, anyway.

According to Seneca, "The greatest remedy for anger is delay." Elinor Dashwood knows this and knows it well.

Furthermore, as the story unfolds, Elinor repeatedly manifests the steps to controlling anger that transcend time and culture. She logically assesses the situation, gets some space, and calmly discusses the issues. If you're facing a difficult circumstance or having to deal with a relative like Harry or people as "charming" as Fanny Dashwood, memorize these steps that Austen has outlined and apply them. You'll be surprised at the blessing and peace they'll bring to your life and to your relationships.

> *An angry man is again angry with himself*
> *when he returns to reason.*
> ~ PUBLILIUS SYRUS ~

Getting Anger Under Control
Logically Assess the Situation

Elinor Dashwood "had an excellent heart; her disposition was affectionate, and her feelings were strong; but she knew how to govern them: it was a knowledge which her mother had yet to learn, and which one of her sisters had resolved never to be taught."[4] Jane Austen makes a monumental statement in this description of Elinor. She assumes that governing the emotions can be taught and learned. Even though Mrs. Henry and Marianne are two of Austen's most flighty characters, she still implies that they *could* learn to govern their emotions if they were taught how.

The same applies to us. Furthermore, the best way to be

taught something is to be shown, not told. Austen does a remarkable job of showing us what self-control looks like in Elinor Dashwood. We are inspired to model her. The novel has barely opened before we see Elinor taking charge of her emotions, logically assessing the situation, stopping her mother from erupting on her stepdaughter-in-law and leaving Norland Park to never return. Elinor first "induced her mother to *reflect* on the propriety of going" and this very action "avoid[s] a breach with [John Dashwood]."[5]

But that's just the start. Elinor continues to logically assess situations as they unfold and remains in control of herself, and thus in control of any anger throughout the novel. Another example occurs when she learns that the man she loves, Edward Ferrars, has been secretly engaged to Lucy Steele while seeming to court her. Elinor realizes Edward has *done her wrong!* At this point, Elinor is a woman scorned—and it's bad enough to warrant a sad, country and western ballad, replete with the equivalent of a verbal volcano:

> *[Elinor's] resentment of such behaviour, her indignation at having been its dupe, for a short time made her feel only for herself; but other ideas, other considerations, soon arose. Had Edward been intentionally deceiving her? Had he feigned a regard for her which he did not feel? Was his engagement to Lucy an engagement of the heart? No: whatever it might once have been, she could not believe it such at present.*[6]

In other words, after Elinor starts out "mortified, shocked, confounded," and mad as a hornet, she allows logic to take over.[7]

And after assessing the situation, Elinor becomes more disturbed for Edward than for herself because she realizes that he must be trapped in an engagement he regrets while being in love with her. Once again, Elinor allows reason to be her guide.

According to Horace, "Anger is a momentary madness, so control your passion or it will control you." We seldom regret the time we allow reason to be our guide. When we pull this off, we usually have nothing to apologize for…nothing to be ashamed of. We've all had times when we've been swayed by our emotions because our mental, emotional, and spiritual growth is a process that lasts a lifetime. But most healthy people strive to make choices based on common sense and logic.

Get Some Space

So many people…so many issues! Difficult people are everywhere. Some people are so obstinate they can't even get along with themselves. Fanny Dashwood is just such a person. Nearly every Jane Austen novel has a "Fanny." I believe Austen created these characters because we can't get through life without meeting a few of them. In *Pride and Prejudice*, it's Lady Catherine de Bourgh (who's "too good" for anyone to even touch). *Mansfield Park* has Aunt Norris. *Northanger Abbey* introduces General Tilney. In *Emma* the difficult person is Augusta Elton. And *Persuasion* has Elizabeth Elliot.

If you think long enough, you can find each of these characters in your own life or recall meeting them. And you usually don't have to know them long before they aggravate you. From there, the temptation to explode can be nearly too great to ignore. Furthermore, sometimes when you do logically assess the situation *they've created*, it just makes you madder because there's no logical reason you should have to put up with their manipulations and issues.

The longer I assess Fanny Dashwood, the less I like her. This woman single-handedly talks her husband out of keeping his promise to his father to monetarily provide for his stepmother and stepsisters. She's the personification of self-seeking and heartlessness. At the first of the novel, the only thing that eases the Dashwood ladies' pain of having to deal with her is the fact that Fanny's brother, Edward, is becoming romantically involved with Elinor.

But soon Elinor's mom gets an invitation from Sir John Middleton to live in Devonshire, and she gladly accepts it. At this point she's put up with Fanny for six months and needs some space in the worst way. Even "Elinor had always thought it would be more prudent for them to settle at some distance from Norland than immediately amongst their present acquaintances."[8] In her wisdom, Elinor knows they need to get away.

Sometimes when we're dealing with difficult people, it's best to get some space. There are some people who are easier to love at a distance, and that's just all there is to it. People like Fanny are out for themselves at all cost. No matter how hard you try, they'll step on you and provoke you to an angry outburst, which will only validate their bad behavior in their own eyes.

There's a Malabar proverb that states, "Anger is as a stone cast into a wasp's nest." Difficult people love to keep the wasp's nest stirred up. They'll throw stones at you in the form of bad attitudes, false accusations, selfish motives, and insults. Not even a saint can hold up to a constant barrage of such abuse.

When Jesus Christ faced an angry mob who planned to throw Him off a cliff, He walked away and left them. Furthermore, He instructed the disciples when sending them out in His name, "If anyone will not welcome you or listen to your words, shake the dust off your feet when you leave that home or town" (Matthew 10:14). There are times to walk away and not look back! Sometimes this is the best course of action—the only course of action that helps us control our anger.

Calmly Discuss the Issues

While we were still remodeling our new ministry headquarters, a stray dog decided our place was home. It's been said that the best dogs are the ones that find you. Well, Lucy found us. And she's a sweet soul who's thrilled to be petted, and she can bark the fear of God into any shadow within a 100-yard radius of the house.

Lucy lived at our ministry site for a couple of months before we moved in. So she was queen of the manor and never imagined that her queenship would be challenged—until the day we moved in and brought over our herd of cats. Yes, five fine furry felines.

Lucy got in her bluff on all of them fairly swiftly. But one of the cats refused to be fooled. That would be Mama Kitty, the queen of the former manor.

Early in her acquaintance with Lucy, Mama Kitty decided she needed to make her position clear. She was queen, and no canine was going to usurp her throne. Mama Kitty repeatedly charged Lucy and ferociously swatted at her. Now understand that Mama Kitty spends 90 percent of her life indoors and has been declawed on her front paws. But Mama Kitty doesn't comprehend this. Neither does Lucy. All it took was a couple of runs and the threat of razor sharp claws from Mama Kitty and Lucy bowed to her royal position. Even though she's six times bigger than Mama Kitty, Lucy has decided not to cross her.

Mama Kitty "discussed" the issues with Lucy, and the two came to an agreement. She rules; Lucy drools. Of course, you have to understand "Cat" to be able to interpret their chat. Nevertheless, they now have an understanding. Any time Mama Kitty goes outside, Lucy gives her all the space she wants and then some.

Sometimes people need to discuss the issues, too. While the threat of claws and a challenging charge might clarify the terms of a cat–dog relationship, people should be more civilized. Unfortunately, they aren't always. I've seen a few conversations between people that resembled a cat fight more than two rational adults discussing issues. Furthermore, sometimes people can treat each other like dogs.

When Jane Austen created Wickham (*Pride and Prejudice*) and Willoughby (*Sense and Sensibility*), she created two guys who, in Elvis' immortal words, "ain't nothin' but a hound dog." She does a fine job of crafting these bad boys with the ability to charm the tail off a cat. They do their share of duping rational women—and a few irrational women as well.

Willoughby sweeps Marianne Dashwood off her feet and comes within a breath of promising her love and matrimony, only to finally dump her. And what a cruel dump it is! In an impersonal letter, he denies having ever been in love with her and states his plans to marry another. This breaks Marianne's heart as badly as if he has died. And once Elinor reads Willoughby's letter,

> *she paused over it for some time with indignant astonishment; then read it again and again; but every perusal only served to increase her abhorrence of the man, and so bitter were her feelings against him, that she dared not trust herself to speak, lest she might wound Marianne still deeper by treating their disengagement, not as a loss to her of any possible good, but as an escape from the worst and most irremediable of evils.*[9]

Early in the book, Austen declares Elinor to be a woman of strong emotions. She certainly fulfills this label after reading Willoughby's letter. Elinor is livid! However, after she has had time to cool down, she is given an opportunity to calmly discuss the situation with Willoughby. During a visit with the Palmers, Marianne indulges in too many walks in the damp countryside and gets so sick the family fears she will die. Willoughby hears of her illness and comes running to discover if she will live. When Elinor finds Willoughby at the door, she acts like Mama Kitty and comes close to hissing at him. Furthermore, she is so vexed she tries to avoid him. But he insists upon talking to her. Finally she listens to his story and suffers only one angry outburst in the middle of it.

As the truth unravels and Elinor realizes that Willoughby has married a woman he does not love for her money alone while his heart belongs to Marianne, her anger dissipates. Even though she is still shocked that Willoughby would abandon a third woman, Eliza, when she was to give birth to his illegitimate child, Elinor still finds herself pitying him. According to Willoughby, he didn't know Eliza was pregnant with his child. However, this illicit affair costs him his inheritance from his relative, Mrs. Smith. Thus he believes he had no other recourse than to marry a wealthy woman he doesn't love…who knows he doesn't love her. Furthermore, he admits that his wife forced him to write the unfeeling letter to Marianne.

After all this spills forth, Elinor sees that the story is much more multifaceted than she had previously understood. She tells Willoughby that he's not as big a scoundrel as she assumed. Furthermore, calmly talking through the issues brings a new peace to Elinor—a deliverance from anger that she would have never received otherwise.

Most of the time when we give an issue time to cool and then calmly discuss the problem with the person who angered us, we discover the same peace and deliverance Elinor experiences. This is a safety valve that stops us from repressing anger. Repressed anger is so volatile it can cause physical, mental, and spiritual illness.

Willoughby's abandoning Marianne and Fanny Dashwood's selfishly cheating the Dashwoods out of an inheritance are issues that happen every day in real life. And when they happen to us or our families, anger is a natural emotion. Even Jesus became so angry with those who were cheating innocent people in the temple that He turned their tables over and scattered money everywhere. Anger is a part of being human. It's what we *do* with the anger that makes the difference.

Scripture states, "In your anger do not sin" (Ephesians 4:6). It's perfectly natural to become angry when we or the ones we love are victims of abuse. Those were the circumstances under which Jesus Christ became angry and the situations in which Elinor found herself and her family. Any time I'm tempted to blow a fuse, I ask myself, "Will this matter in 100 years?" If it won't, I figure it's not worth my anger now. If it *will* matter in 100 years, then I do my best to wisely handle the anger in a manner that will not violate love and, therefore, fulfill my quest of regret-free living.

Remember, you don't have to live a lifestyle of anger and conflict in any relationship. You can take control, set boundaries, and find freedom.

> *Anybody can become angry—that is easy;*
> *but to be angry with the right person, and to the right*
> *degree, and at the right time, and for the right purpose,*
> *and in the right way—that is not*
> *within everybody's power and is not easy.*
> ~ Aristotle ~

1. Jane Austen, *Sense and Sensibility*, The Complete Novels of Jane Austen, vol. I (New York: The Modern Library, 1992), p. 5.
2. Ibid., p. 4.
3. Ibid., p. 6.
4. Ibid., p. 5.
5. Ibid., p. 5.
6. Ibid., p. 97.
7. Ibid., p. 97.
8. Ibid., p. 18.
9. Ibid., p. 129.

Love keeps no record of wrongs...

Henry Tilney and the Sphinx

The remedy for wrongs is to forget them.
~ Publilius Syrus ~

During one ministry trip our family was blessed to visit Mt. Rushmore. While we were looking at the faces of those great men carved in stone, we had a discussion about how wonderfully the sculptures have held up. From our vantage point, there was little or no evidence of erosion. All the carved features were still well-defined and sharp.

I said something like, "When you think about the effects of acid rain on the Greek structures in Athens, I wonder how long the presidents will stay in this good shape?"

Daniel said, "Yeah, that's something to think about."

I said, "But you know, the sphinx still looks pretty good considering it's been around for more than 4500 years."

"What's the sphinx?" my daughter, Brooke, asked. She was about seven at the time.

"Oh, I know," Brett chimed in. He was nine and really wanted to show off his vast knowledge. He and I explained to Brooke that the great sphinx was a big cat person statue in Egypt.

After that conversation, we walked around the rest of the national park, took in the sights, saw a mountain goat or two, and had fun.

Well, the day wore on and we began to get a little tired. We decided to go into the gift and snack shop and purchase some ice-cream cones. At places like this you pay about ten bucks a scoop for ice cream. Okay, it wasn't quite that expensive, but it was enough to consider floating a small loan. But I'll never forget the taste of that purple boysenberry ice cream as we sat there as a family, reminisced about the day so far, and shared some laughter.

The shop had floor-to-ceiling windows at the entry, and I was sitting with my back to the windows. Daniel was sitting across from me and looking out the windows. Soon he said, "Looks like some clouds are moving in. I wonder if it's going to rain?"

I turned around and looked over my shoulder at a bank of dark, threatening clouds that were trailing across the sky above the stone presidents. I said, "Well, the sphinx has been around a long time," and turned back to Daniel.

For some strange reason, a blank, confused expression cloaked his features. He stopped the assault on his ice cream and said, "What?"

The kids started giggling.

I couldn't imagine what the deal was and why he hadn't

followed me. "The sphinx!" I insisted. "It's been around a long time."

"Well, what does that have to do with what I said?"

"Acid rain," I explained and realized I'd left a major section of my thought process out of the conversation. I started laughing out loud.

Daniel joined in. The kids were now fully seized by hilarity.

"When you said it was going to rain," I explained, "I thought, 'It's going to rain on the presidents' faces, and if it's acid rain then that will contribute to the erosion process.' Since that concerns me, I comforted myself with, 'Well, the sphinx has been around a long time.' And that's what I said to you." My laughter increased. "What's the deal? Why didn't you follow all that?" I teased.

"I have no earthly idea," Daniel said and rolled his eyes.

Brett sat straight up and mimicked my husband and me. His head bobbing from side to side, he said, "Hmmm…looks like it's going to rain…Yeah, and the sphinx has been around a long time."

By this point we were laughing so loud everyone in the shop was staring at us like we were nuts. But we didn't care. We were having the time of our lives. That was a family moment we will never forget.

Unfortunately, that's what having a conversation with me can be like. My mind often hops from one concept or subject to the next, and I don't necessarily bother to inform the person I'm having a conversation with that there's a subject change or that I'm leaving out a wealth of details that tumbled through my brain.

Now, after that incident at Mt. Rushmore, any time any of us does that to the other, we say, "You sphinxed me!"

When I created Kathy Moore in *Northpointe Chalet* (based on *Northanger Abbey*), I made her a bit wackier than Austen's Catherine Morland. She's the kind of person who would sphinx you on a regular basis. Even though Catherine Morland isn't quite as scatterbrained as my Kathy, I'm sure there are times in *Northanger Abbey* when Henry Tilney feels sphinxed—not so much conversationally but definitely in some of the unexpected things she does. Unfortunately, one of Catherine's unexpected antics could have destroyed her relationship with Henry had he not been so ready to forgive and forget.

Catherine, a young lady with a fanciful mind, lets her imagination run wild. She has a love affair with Gothic romances—the darker the better. So she looks for a mystery under every rock and finds murderous clues where none exist. Catherine goes on a snooping expedition because she decides that Henry Tilney's father murdered his wife.

> "And may I not, in my turn," said [Henry], as he pushed back the folding doors, "ask how you came here?…"
>
> "I have been," said Catherine, looking down, "to see your mother's room."
>
> "My mother's room! Is there anything extraordinary to be seen there?"

"No, nothing at all…"

"As there is nothing in the room in itself to raise curiosity, this must have proceeded from a sentiment of respect for my mother's character, as described by Eleanor, which does honour to her memory. The world, I believe, never saw a better woman….[My father] loved her, I am persuaded, as well as it was possible for him to…"

"I am very glad of it," said Catherine; "it would have been very shocking—"

"If I understand you rightly, you had formed a surmise of such horror as I have hardly words to—Dear Miss Morland, consider the dreadful nature of the suspicions you have entertained. What have you been judging from? Remember the country and the age in which we live. Remember that we are English: that we are Christians. Consult your own understanding, your own sense of the probable, your own observation of what is passing around you. Does our education prepare us for such atrocities? Do our laws connive at them? Could they be perpetrated without being known in a country like this, where social and literary intercourse is on such a footing, where every man is surrounded by a neighbourhood of voluntary spies, and where roads and newspapers lay everything open? Dearest Miss Morland, what ideas have you been admitting?"

They had reached the end of the gallery; and with tears of shame she ran off to her own room.[1]

In this famous scene from *Northanger Abbey*, Henry Tilney very eloquently asks Catherine Morland if she's nuts. While she isn't nuts, Catherine is young and impressionable, and Tilney Sr.

is a callous grouch. When Tilney's gruff nature meets Catherine's wild imagination, the natural result is to turn him into a killer who murdered his wife. That means Catherine is accusing her possible future father-in-law of being a murderer. Not so good for family relations or a budding romance!

Catherine is plunged into a piteous state when she realizes all her imaginary ramblings have been uncovered, and they are shamefully erroneous. Unfortunately, her mental musings don't result in the hilarity that my "sphinxing" did. Fortunately, Jane Austen pairs Catherine with a gracious man who keeps no record of wrongs.

First Corinthians doesn't say that love doesn't *remember* wrongs. I'm sure no man would ever forget if his girlfriend accused his innocent father of murder. The issue is that love keeps *no record* of wrongs. The *reason* a person would keep a record is what's important.

First, records are often kept for a point of reference that can be reviewed, evaluated, and weighed. The event or situation kept can be mulled over and be a source for bitterness, unforgiveness, and, if given half a chance, a reason for retaliation. Like an accountant keeps a record of bills owed, so those who hold a grudge keep a record of wrongs done to them in order to plan for revenge.

Second, this process enables the victim to nurture a grudge like a gardener might nurture prized vegetables. The more the person reviews the record of the wrong, the bigger that grudge grows, and the more consuming it becomes.

Furthermore, the record-keeping person stays in victim

mode. Harboring a mental record of wrongs allows him to continue to view himself as the injured one. While love is freeing, viewing oneself as a victim is bondage.

> *Humanity is never so beautiful as when praying for forgiveness, or else forgiving another.*
> ~ JEAN PAUL RICHTER ~

A Reason to Retaliate

If Henry had kept a record of Catherine's mistake and allowed it to affect his opinion of her or drive him to retaliation, he would have ended any chance for their relationship to grow. When we keep records of wrongs and use that list as a reason to retaliate, we are expending energies we should tap into for personal growth...maybe even survival. And if the retaliation mind-set or process consumes us, we can lose our ability to find a new birth. Even the most scarred relationships can find that new life when both parties choose to keep no record of wrongs and put the past behind them.

Up until the point that Henry realizes that Catherine's imagination has turned his father into a murderer, he actually has an indulgent view of her preoccupation with Gothic novels. When they are traveling to the abbey, he encourages her to imagine all sorts of scenarios that involve mysterious furniture, a haunted chamber, a wicked storm, and a series of subterraneous rooms that feature blood, a dagger, and an unthinkable instrument of torture. While Henry is laughing at Catherine, he doesn't realize that her wild imagination will actually invent similar scenarios or that he'll get aggravated at her because of her conjuring.

Once Henry does realize his error and confronts Catherine, she is thrown into a tailspin of worries about his holding the offense against her:

> It was not only with herself that she was sunk, but with Henry. Her folly, which now seemed even criminal, was all exposed to him, and he must despise her for ever. The liberty which her imagination had dared to take with the character of his father, could he ever forgive it? The absurdity of her curiosity and her fears, could they ever be forgotten? She hated herself more than she could express.[2]

But soon Catherine realizes she has no reason to worry. The next time she sees Henry, he shows her more attention than ever and comforts her with "soothing politeness."[3]

Why? Because that's the stuff love is made of. In the face of disillusionment and exasperation, love comes through to offer forgiveness and a balm to a hurting soul. Henry Tilney wins my "Most Forgiving Hero Award."

Nurturing a Grudge

When I wrote my modern-day version of *Northanger Abbey* (called *Northpointe Chalet*), I changed the dynamics of the plot a bit. In the original work Henry's father rejects Catherine because he learns that Catherine is not wealthy, as he originally assumed. However, in my book I have Zachariah Tilman (my General Tilney) discover Kathy Moore snooping in his deceased wife's room. This results in a huge confrontation in which Kathy admits she is trying to prove he killed his wife. Tilman calls Kathy a two-faced liar and forbids her from coming back on his property. In reality, Zachariah Tilman, gruff as he might be, is a grieving widower who loved his wife. Kathy's entering his wife's room and reading her diary are desecrations he cannot tolerate or forgive.

As a result, Ben Tilman (my Henry) decides to break off the relationship with Kathy—not because he holds a grudge against her but because his father does. Ben doesn't want his in-law relations to be as stormy as those in his family of origin. And he sees that it can and will be, given his father's grudge against Kathy.

"I don't like this any more than you do, Kathy!"

"Then why go through with it?" she demanded and lifted both hands like a lawyer in her final argument.

"Because my father can't stand you!" he explained, his voice even and hard…

"If you really cared for me, Ben, you'd tell your dad to take a hike!" She doubled her fists at her sides.

"Maybe breaking up with you is a greater act of love than staying with you," Ben defended. "Do you really want to spend the rest of your life dealing with him?"

"No, I don't!" Kathy said. "But I wouldn't have to, would

I? Why couldn't you just tell him to stay out of our lives? Break up with him instead of me!"

"Do you want to break up with your parents?"

Ben's staccato words rendered Kathy speechless.

"Put yourself in my position, why don't you?" He stood and scooted the stool aside. It growled against the exposed wood and teetered to a stop… "My father's not always right. He's done some things really wrong. But I will tell you that he's worked like a dog for our family. He was there for me when I was a kid. I can't just ditch him in his retirement years. I at least owe him some loyalty, don't I?"[4]

Any time we keep a record of wrongs, nurturing a grudge is a given. A grudge is like a big, hairy monster that takes over our minds and inserts its tentacles into every nook and crevice of our lives. Eventually, we don't hold the grudge—the grudge holds us. Finally we *become* the grudge. Our minds are consumed with the memories of what has happened, the resulting pain, and the desire to forever feed the pain, the memories, and the temptations to retaliate.

In the final stage of consumption, the grudge destroys relationships—even between those who don't hold the grudge. In *Northpointe Chalet*, Ben temporarily ends his relationship with Kathy because his father holds a grudge against her. The son and potential daughter-in-law are negatively impacted by the sins of the father. And the father, a bitter control freak, doesn't have a healthy relationship with anyone—not even his own daughter because of his penchant for harboring negative emotions.

However, as with Henry and Catherine, love conquers all. At the end of *Northpointe Chalet* the hero gets his lady. Ben and Kathy become engaged. Ben doesn't break up with his father, but he and Kathy put some boundaries on their interactions with him and his grudges.

Unless you're blessed with a heavy dose of amnesia, you can never forget something bad that happens. The deep wounds and hard injuries become part of the tapestry of your past and color who you are and what you become. But with God's grace and healing, we can remember without the pain or the desire to harbor a grudge.

Staying in the Victim Mode

When we keep a record of wrongs, it allows us to remain victims. We can perpetually mull over the list of sins committed against us and howl about them any time we choose. Soon our identity is tangled in the wrongs committed against us. And since the person who holds the grudge eventually *becomes* the grudge, so we can irrevocably *become* victims.

Interestingly enough, sometimes the wrongs committed can be things we've done to ourselves. We become victims of our own wrong choices. And just as we can wallow in "victimville" over things others have done to us, we can also roll around in the mistakes we've made and circumstances we've brought upon ourselves.

For instance Catherine Morland (in *Northanger Abbey*) is guilty of accusing an innocent man of a murder. As a result,

Henry Tilney severely reproaches her. Then Catherine is thrown into a valley of regrets that essentially leads to a "How could I have been so daft?" soliloquy.

However, after Catherine "made herself as miserable as possible for about half an hour," she decides to go downstairs and do the inevitable—face Henry. In the midst of his generosity and good conduct, Catherine does what we all must do in order to climb out of the victim state…she forgives. In her case, it's herself she must forgive.

Whether it is ourselves or another, the strength that's developed through forgiveness provides the courage and fortitude we need to drag ourselves out of victim mode and into recovery. Continually going over the record of wrongs that have been done to us is equivalent to tightening the chains of bondage with every recitation. While it's never healthy to ignore abusive behavior and allow ourselves or enable ourselves to be repeatedly victimized, leaving the past in the past is the only means to victorious living.

> *The weak can never forgive. Forgiveness is*
> *the attribute of the strong.*
> ~ MAHATMA GANDHI ~

1. Jane Austen, *Northanger Abbey*, The Complete Novels of Jane Austen, vol. II (New York: The Modern Library, 1992), pp. 487-89.

2. Ibid., p. 489.

3. Ibid., p. 490.

4. Debra White Smith, *Northpointe Chalet* (Eugene, OR: Harvest House, 2005), pp. 310-11.

Love does not delight in evil but rejoices with the truth…

10

Anne Elliot and the Black Heart

You will know the truth, and the truth will set you free.
~ John 8:32 ~

If there are two words that may at first appear to be the opposite of each other it is truth and evil. We always think of truth as pure, sparkling, and forever freeing while evil is dark, sinister, and the stuff that bondage is made of. However, sometimes truth and evil go hand in hand.

Even though discovering truth is freeing, sometimes it is ugly. Uncovering the truth might lead to evil facts…or the realization that a person we thought we could trust is bad. Even in such cases, the knowledge of how things really are has the uncanny ability to bring us freedom. And even if the truth reveals an evil plot or design or character, we can rejoice in knowing the truth because it arms us with the defense of not placing our trust where it will be violated.

Salvador was a successful businessman whom many people admired. But for every person who admired him, there were scores who envied his successes. One person in particular envied Salvador, but he had no idea the person had negative feelings toward him. Ironically, Salvador thought of that person as one of his best friends and loved him like a brother…and served him like a brother.

Tragically, Salvador overheard a conversation in which his best friend slammed him and indicated that he barely tolerated Salvador. At first, he was deeply hurt. After all, he viewed the guy as a close friend and thought his love was returned when, in reality, it was not.

After Salvador got over the initial pain, he realized his friend had never been very supportive. Salvador had done most of the giving in their relationship. His friend had been in charge of taking and "tolerating." Finally, Salvador understood that the man was eaten up with envy because of his successes and would never be a true friend.

Even though this truth initially hurt Salvador, he eventually rejoiced in it. After he'd grieved the loss of the friendship, he was glad that he'd learned the truth. While he didn't delight in his friend's evil thoughts, he was glad that he'd discovered the truth before the one-sided friendship rocked on a few more years. The truth set Salvador free from a dysfunctional relationship.

In *Persuasion*, Anne Elliot is being pursued by a man whose character she questions. Even though she is not as duped by him as Salvador was by his friend, Anne still doesn't know everything about Mr. Elliot's intentions. Only after a visit to her friend, Mrs. Smith, does Anne encounter the complete truth:

> *"I beg your pardon, my dear Miss Elliot," [Mrs. Smith] cried in her natural tone of cordiality, "I beg your pardon for the short answers I have been giving you, but I have been uncertain what I ought to do...However, I have determined; I think I am right; I think you ought to be made acquainted with Mr. Elliot's real character. Though I fully believe that at present you have not the smallest intention of accepting him, there is no saying what may happen. You might, some time or other, be differently affected towards him. Hear the truth, therefore, now, while you are unprejudiced. Mr. Elliot is a man without heart or conscience; a designing, wary cold-blooded being, who thinks only of himself; who, for his own interest or ease, would be guilty of any cruelty, or any treachery, that could be perpetrated without risk of his general character. He has no feeling for others. Those whom he has been the chief cause of leading into ruin, he can neglect and desert without the smallest compunction. He is totally beyond the reach of any sentiment of justice or compassion. Oh! he is black at heart; hollow and black!"* [1]

There is nothing so freeing as hearing what you've suspected confirmed. The doubts are over. The truth is unveiled. And even if it is negative, we are free from the questions that plague us in regard to the issues or individuals. Unfortunately, many good people who have information that will bring enlightenment to a negative situation often hesitate to extend that information. Like Mrs. Smith, they are afraid if they say the truth they'll look like gossips or sound like they're slamming the party involved. As a result, the truth is never told.

I think many well-intentioned people struggle with telling the truth when it will make someone look bad. But sometimes the truth needs to be told, even if it is ugly and will reveal evil. When self-seeking people are allowed to prey on others while people in the know hide the truth about those people's natures, then the person hiding truth becomes a party to the evil.

> *A person may cause evil to others not only by his actions but by his inaction, and in either case he is justly accountable to them for the injury.*
> ~ JOHN STUART MILL ~

Telling the Truth

Lorna had a negative experience with Susan. To put it bluntly, Susan was a control freak who couldn't take anyone doing anything she didn't approve of. On top of that, she was in a position of leadership. Susan was the women's ministries director at her church and was in charge of an event that involved several churches. Lorna volunteered to help with the event, and that's where the trouble started.

Lorna was a take-charge kind of person who worked well on her own. She even owned her own business. After a week of sacrificial work and hard labor on behalf of the women's ministry event, Lorna asked Susan about the flower arrangement setup. Susan told Lorna where each arrangement should go.

Lorna, used to working for herself, made some alterations

to the flower arrangement placements. In her mind the changes brought an improvement, and she figured Susan would logically assess the situation and agree. Her intent and her heart were to improve the decorating, not go against what Susan said.

When Susan looked at the flower arrangements, it was obvious they were not placed in exactly the places she had outlined. Being the control person she was, Susan exploded into rage at Lorna. On top of that, she treated Lorna like a misbehaving child rather than an adult of equal value and intellect.

Lorna wasn't the type to lie down when verbally attacked. She stood her ground, which finally ended in her marching off in one direction and Susan stomping away in the other. All Lorna could think after the encounter was *I can't believe this woman is going into such a fury over, of all things, flower arrangements!*

But finally she speculated that perhaps the whole thing wasn't really about flower arrangements, maybe it was about control. Lorna suspected that Susan was so insecure she couldn't take anyone doing anything in a way she had not dictated. Furthermore, Lorna deduced that Susan possibly viewed what she'd done as the grossest of insubordination, which was the wrong attitude to have against someone who had sacrificially served at a ministry event.

Once this realization hit her, Lorna decided to conduct her own little investigation. Her primary purpose was to see if perhaps the whole ordeal should be attributed to Susan's control tendencies, or if Lorna should view herself partially in the wrong. She wanted to be completely honest with herself and didn't want to foist blame on Susan if she should take responsibility for what happened. However, her gut instinct insisted that Susan was the problem, and that she'd overreacted beyond reason. Lorna wanted validation for her assumptions.

So she had a conversation with someone that Susan attended church with. She mentioned that she'd had a negative interaction with Susan and wanted to know if Susan created problems at her church as well. Interestingly enough, the lady, Becky, hedged around the question. She was a good, Christian woman who didn't want to be involved in giving a bad report, so she was non-committal. When Lorna slightly pressed for a definite answer, she said, "No, Susan does not cause any problems at church."

Being the intuitive sort, Lorna backed off but realized that Becky had probably not told the truth. Becky lied to not look like a gossip. Therefore, Lorna approached Becky again and apologized for perhaps making her feel pressured, but explained that she'd had a very negative experience with Susan and she wanted to make certain that it wasn't just her.

At that point Becky revealed the truth. Yes, there were significant problems at church. Susan created negative situation after situation. However, Becky hadn't wanted to put Susan down because Susan did do some things right. Lorna thanked Becky and went away very much at peace and very free from the guilt trip Susan had tried to shove upon her. She also pledged to avoid working with Susan.

The truth brought freedom. Lorna rejoiced in it. She didn't delight in the fact that Susan evidently had a dark, controlling side. But knowing the truth gave her peace and the wisdom to avoid a future confrontation.

A similar dynamic happens in *Persuasion*. When Anne Elliot goes to visit her friend Mrs. Smith, the lady hedges in revealing condemning information about Mr. Elliot. He is Anne's cousin who has matrimonial designs on her. Mrs. Smith starts the conversation by actually complimenting Mr. Elliot because she believes that he and Anne are soon to be engaged. However, once Anne makes it clear that she has no intention of marrying Mr. Elliot, Mrs. Smith finally tells the truth about him: "He is totally beyond the reach of any sentiment of justice or compassion. Oh! he is black at heart; hollow and black!"[2] Because of her willingness to tell the truth, the whole truth, and nothing but the truth in the face of fearing the consequences, I give Mrs. Smith the "Bravely Honest Award."

Like Lorna, Anne is thankful to hear the truth, even though it reveals Mr. Elliot's money-hungry, self-centered nature. Her suspicions of his true nature are confirmed by Mrs. Smith's gutsy recounting of how he has ill-used his family as well as her. And Anne assures Mrs. Smith that she is thankful for her honesty: "You have asserted nothing contradictory to what Mr. Elliot appeared to be some years ago. This is all in confirmation, rather, of what we used to hear and believe."[3]

And just as truth armed Lorna with the best mode of action (avoiding Susan), this knowledge arms Anne with how to deal with Mr. Elliot. "I am very glad to know all this," said Anne, after a little thoughtfulness. "It will be more painful to me in some respects to be in company with him, but I shall know better what to do. My line of conduct will be more direct. Mr. Elliot is evidently a disingenuous, artificial, worldly man, who has had never any better principle to guide him than selfishness."[4]

According to James Russell Lowell, "The greatest homage we can pay to truth is to use it." Covering evil is a form of participating in it. Even though we need to use tact and be sensitive to the feelings and situations of those involved when revealing truth, sometimes being purely honest in a negative situation takes more guts than remaining silent. And when telling the truth unveils gross dysfunction, it can lead to the truth-bearer being ostracized from family and friends who don't want the truth. According to Richard Whately, "Everyone wishes to have truth on his side, but not everyone wishes to be on the side of truth." However, telling the truth is one of the most responsible and enlightening things we can do.

Delighting in Evil…or the Latest Juicy Tidbit

The basis of gossip involves delighting in evil. The latest juicy detail is savored and jumped on. The bearer can't wait to repeat it. The information often comes through a line of several people who repeat and perhaps add their interpretation to the situation. None of these people investigate to see if the information is true. Gossips readily and gladly share what they've learned. It can be a way of life for them, and they are a never-ending flow of negative information about anyone and everyone. This is the nature of gossip.

Even though Anne Elliot believes everything Mrs. Smith says

about Mr. Elliot's nature, she hesitates to believe that Mr. Elliot is planning to propose to her. The reason she believes one set of information and not the other is directly related to the way Mrs. Smith receives the information. Regarding Mr. Elliot's character, Mrs. Smith discovers those truths firsthand by observation, what he has told her and his treatment of her. She even has evidence in a letter written by him that he once disdained Anne's father and family. However, when it comes to the tidbit about Mr. Elliot's planning to marry Anne, the information doesn't come firsthand. Mrs. Smith herself admits, "It takes a bend or two."[5]

The "bend or two" involves Colonel Wallis telling his wife, who tells her nurse, Mrs. Rooke. Mrs. Rooke is a good friend to Mrs. Smith, and, therefore, tells all to Mrs. Smith. After telling Mrs. Smith her "authority is deficient,"[6] Anne says, "Indeed, Mrs. Smith, we must not expect to get real information in such a line. Facts or opinions which are to pass through the hands of so many, to be misconceived by folly in one, and ignorance in another, can hardly have much truth left."[7]

However, Anne does give Mrs. Smith the respect of hearing her out. And, in this case, Mrs Smith is correct about Mr. Elliot. But in most cases when information has been passed from one person to another to another, the final version is incorrect.

One of the things I've learned through the years is, like Anne Elliot, to ask the source of the information. If the tidbit bearer tells me it came from someone who is known for gossip, I usually dismiss the details as error. I also dismiss the information as error if there is a "bend or two" in the way the information came to me. Very rarely will the information be correct, as it is in Mrs. Smith's recitation of Mr. Elliot's intent to marry Anne.

Another clue that often tips me that the information is gossip involves the teller's attitude. Gossips *love* "sharing." However, when someone hesitates to state the facts, as did Becky when telling the truth about Susan, chances are higher that they are revealing the facts. Although love rejoices in the truth, it can also grieve when having to reveal a truth that is going to cause pain or make a loved one look bad—even if he or she really is bad. Those who delight in evil or the latest juicy tidbit *enjoy* the whole process.

Finally, remember that time often reveals truth. So before repeating something, it's best to allow time to reveal if it's truth or error. According to William Cullen Bryant, "Truth gets well if she is run over by a locomotive, while error dies of lockjaw if she scratches her finger."

> *It is easier to perceive error than to find truth,*
> *for the former lies on the surface and is easily seen, while*
> *the latter lies in the depth, where few are*
> *willing to search for it.*
> ~ JOHANNE WOLFGANG VON GOETHE ~

1. Jane Austen, *Persuasion*, The Complete Novels of Jane Austen, vol. II (New York: The Modern Library, 1992), pp. 671-72.

2. Ibid., p. 672.

3. Ibid., p. 674.

4. Ibid., p. 679.

5. Ibid., p. 676.

6. Ibid.

7. Ibid., p. 677.

Love always protects…

⌒11⌒

Elizabeth Bennet and the Selfless Secret

Love gives itself; it is not bought.
~ Henry Wadsworth Longfellow ~

When I wrote the Jane Austen fiction series for Harvest House Publishers, the first book I wrote was based on *Pride and Prejudice*. It seemed fitting to start with that book since that was the first Austen book I read. Creating the vibrant relationship between Darcy and Elizabeth was quite enjoyable, mainly because the sparks fly between those two from the minute they see each other. There is an electric attraction between the sexes that is fun to write about, and it's evident in the Darcy/Elizabeth dynamic.

One of the elements I enjoyed retelling most is the part where Darcy secretively assists Lydia. His initial driving force is his love for Elizabeth and his desire to protect her sister and her family's reputation. In my book *First Impressions*, the translation from the turn of the nineteenth century to the turn of the twenty-first century wrought a slightly different plot. In *Pride and Prejudice*, Lydia and Wickham run off together and scandalously live together out of wedlock with Wickham having no intention of marrying. In *First Impressions*, Dave Davidson (my Darcy) is driven by his love for Eddi Boswick (my Elizabeth), when he intervenes in her sister's life. Linda (my Lydia) and Rick (my Wickham) have an affair, and the result is an unwanted pregnancy. In the minds of these irresponsible young adults, there is only one choice: abortion.

Both Eddi and her other sister, Jenny, are distraught. Rick discovers the story when Eddi is attending church and steps to the altar during family prayer time. He watches as her shoulders shake with her weeping. Knowing Eddi isn't a woman who cries easily, Dave understands there's something dreadfully wrong. Despite their estranged relationship, he is moved to her side to discover the problem. Once she tells him everything, Dave is then driven to act on her behalf because he loves her and wants to protect her, her family, and her sister from the same type of pain that Rick Wallace has dealt him.

So Dave goes to Rick's apartment, where he finds Linda, and discovers what Linda really wants to do with her child.

> "So...let's just pretend I really am your summer Santa..." Dave said, infusing every word with kindness and hope, "...what would be your very first choice in all this?"
>
> Linda observed Dave as if he were a fairy she'd stopped

believing in years ago, and now she'd discovered he really did exist. "Are you saying you'll make it happen?" she asked.

"I'm saying I'll make it happen," Dave affirmed.

"Okay, then." Linda looked into Dave's soul. "If you really think you could make it happen then…what I wanted to do at first was, well," she shrugged, "you know, get married."

"That's exactly what I figured," Dave asserted.

"Rick says that's old-fashioned," Linda said with a sad smile.

Dave stood. "It's called doing the decent thing," he growled…

Linda looked at Dave as if he really were her fairy. "You mean you're going to—"

"I'm going to make Rick Wallace do what's right, and I'm going to make sure he treats you like a queen."

"But wh–why?" Linda gasped. "You don't even know me."

"Because I know your sister," Dave said and marched down the short hallway. And I love your sister, *he added to himself.*[1]

The same protective love that motivates Dave Davidson also motivates Darcy. When Lydia runs off with Wickham, Darcy secretively steps forward to make sure Wickham does the honorable thing. This is even after Elizabeth has turned down Darcy's proposal, chewed him out, and told him he is the most egocentric person she's ever met. Nevertheless, love will not be denied. Just like Dave, Darcy must protect his love by protecting Lydia and her family's reputation. When Elizabeth learns the truth in a letter from her aunt, she is as blown away:

The contents of this letter threw Elizabeth into a flutter of spirits, in which it was difficult to determine whether pleasure or pain bore the greatest share…[Darcy] had followed [Lydia and Wickham] purposefully to town, he had taken on himself all the trouble and mortification attendant on such as research; in which supplication had been necessary to a woman whom he must abominate and despise, and where he was reduced to meet—frequently meet, reason with, persuade, and finally bribe—the man whom he always most wished to avoid, and whose very name it was punishment to him to pronounce. He had done all this for a girl whom he could neither regard nor esteem. [Elizabeth's] heart did whisper that he had done it for her. But it was a hope shortly checked by other considerations, and she soon felt that even her vanity was insufficient, when required to depend on his affection for her, for a woman who had already refused him…It was painful, exceedingly painful, to know that they were under obligations to such a person who could never receive a return. They owed the restoration of Lydia, her character, everything to him. Oh! how heartily did she grieve over every ungracious sensation she had ever encouraged, every saucy speech she had ever directed towards him. For herself, she was humbled; but she was proud of him. Proud that in a cause of compassion and honor he had been able to get the better of himself. She read over her aunt's commendation of him again and again. It was hardly enough; but it pleased her. She was even sensible of some pleasure, though mixed with regret, on finding how steadfastly both she and her uncle had been persuaded that affection and confidence subsisted between Mr. Darcy and herself.[2]

Whether in the nineteenth century or the twenty-first century, love always protects. That is part of what love is made of. That's why I've given Darcy the "Most Selfless Award." True love is selfless and thinks of the other person before the self. This quality of love views situations from the other person's viewpoint. And from this vantage, love chooses what is best for the one loved, not what is best for the self. When this level of love is manifested, every relationship it is released into is transformed, whether a marriage, a friendship, or a parent–child relationship.

> *To love is to place our happiness in the*
> *happiness of another.*
> ~ GOTTFRIED WILHELM VON LEIBNITZ ~

Love Views Situations from the Other Person's Viewpoint

When my writing career took off, my son was three and Daniel and I were in the process of adopting our daughter. By the time we went to Vietnam and brought our daughter home, Brett was four and my daughter was nearly two. They were at an age that required a lot from me. And I was happy to give to them. At the same time, my writing had opened up numerous doors for me to speak at women's events and writers' conferences. From the start, I had a very deep sense that I should put firm boundaries on my schedule. I knew some speakers were gone nearly every weekend, and I didn't want to take the chance of that happening.

Even though the prospect of being booked to speak every weekend was quite exciting to me, I projected myself to my kids' viewpoint and disconnected from self-interest. From there, I viewed my career. What I saw and felt were a couple of little ones who wanted their mother and wanted her most of the time. Therefore, with God's leading, I limited my speaking engagements to once a month.

Being gone once a month turned out to be therapeutic for both the kids and me. Even though my writing schedule was full, I was still a stay-at-home mom since I worked from my home. I was with my kids most of the time. After awhile, most moms start needing a break, and I was no exception. Being gone one to two nights every month was beneficial for me and the kids. They appreciated me more when I got back home, and I was able to be a better mom because I got a break and enjoyed some "me time" in a hotel room. It also gave my kids some special quality time with Daniel.

Now my kids are turning 10 and 12. They are growing up fast. Looking back, I am beyond thankful that I looked at my life from their viewpoint. I have no regrets. I was there for them when they skinned their knees. I blew bubbles and took them to the park. I swam with them and played ball. I corrected them when they needed it. Best of all, I was the woman they needed. I was their full-time mom.

Putting yourself in the other person's shoes requires that

you totally disconnect from self-love and self-interest and make your mind view a situation the way the other person sees it. This requires a willingness to admit that we might not have all the answers or always be right. People who aren't willing to do this usually believe that everyone else is wrong and they are right. From this standpoint, they refuse to apologize or make amends. After all, it's hard to apologize when you believe you're never in the wrong.

If I had believed this, I would have taken every speaking opportunity that came up and believed I was right to do that. If my family complained or objected, I would have blamed them for complaining and viewed filling *my* schedule as *my* prerogative. But true love doesn't do that. True love protects. I chose to protect my kids from the possibility of my career robbing them of the one woman they needed most in the world—their mom. (My husband has made these same choices with his career.)

When Darcy chose to arrange for Lydia to marry Wickham, he did it because he put himself in Elizabeth's shoes and viewed the situation from her standpoint. As far as he was concerned, Lydia was a flighty 15-year-old who threw herself at soldiers, and Wickham was a low-life scoundrel who took advantage of young things—especially if they had money. Since Lydia didn't have any money, he took what she offered—her virginity. Darcy already couldn't stand the thought of Wickham because Wickham had romanced his sister with the intent of taking her fortune. As for Lydia, Darcy could have easily thought, *That's what she gets for throwing herself at men.* Instead, he set aside his own opinions and acted on what was best for Elizabeth, her family, and Lydia. He protected the woman he loved from the social scandal that would have occurred if everyone learned of Lydia's folly. And he did this in the face of disdaining Wickham.

Love Chooses What Is Best for the One Loved

After my kids got older I accepted more frequent speaking engagements for a few years. Soon I realized that my being gone was beginning to wear thin with all of us. So my husband and I made the decision to keep our family together. Any existing bookings I had, I asked permission to bring my family and, for the most part, absorbed the cost of them traveling with me. For any new bookings, I explained that we were a family-of-four package deal. My husband and I also started offering special music at the ministry events.

Because of this decision, I've had some groups who have declined booking me. Ironically, I've been criticized for my choice by a few, and my husband has had some women be rude to him. I've lost money because some small groups can't afford for all of us to come. A few times we've paid for our own travel expenses or come for a love offering. A time or two I've gone in the red. And sometimes we just break even. My decision has cost us a significant number of bookings as well as hard, cold cash.

However, now that we've been doing this several years, I'm looking back and am as thankful I've made this sacrifice as I was when I limited my solo travel to once-a-month. We've had some remarkable times together. My kids have seen numerous national parks and much of the United States. Even in the face of losing some bookings, we've still had enough engagements that we've stayed as busy as we need to be.

I have no regrets. It was best for our family and my kids for us to stay together. And selfless love chooses what's best for the object of that love.

Now that my kids are entering their preteen and teen years, they are growing more and more independent. And my husband and I are realizing that there will be some upcoming ministry events that I book solo again. And again I'll keep those solo events to a limited number a year while continuing to travel with my family because that is what's best for our kids.

Just as my choices have cost me, so Darcy's choice to assist Lydia and protect Elizabeth cost him. When Lydia won't hear of leaving Wickham, Darcy begins to take financial measures to essentially bribe Wickham to marry Lydia. According to Elizabeth's Aunt Gardiner, "[Wickham's] debts are to be paid, amounting, I believe to considerably more than a thousand pounds, another thousand in addition to her own settled upon her and his commission purchased."[3] A thousand pounds at the turn of the nineteenth century is equivalent to about $30,000 to $40,000 now. Darcy paid between $60,000 and $80,000 up front. One half to pay off Wickham's debts and the other half to provide a cash settlement for Wickham to marry Lydia. And Lydia would receive a small, yearly settlement of her own from her family. Furthermore, since Darcy clears Wickham's debt, he will not be forced to resign his commission, as he'd originally planned. So he has that income as well.

To further underscore Darcy's selflessness, understand that he has no intention of Elizabeth ever learning what he has done. His motives are pure. There is no ulterior thinking: *I'll rescue Lydia and Elizabeth will see what a great guy I am, change her mind about me, fall in love with me, and be glad to marry me.* Me…me…me! No, Darcy doesn't even think in these terms.

Instead, he selflessly takes responsibility for what he believes is partly his fault. According to Aunt Gardiner, "The reason why all this was to be done by [Darcy] alone was such as I have given above. It was owing to him, to his reserve and want of proper consideration, that Wickham's character had been so misunderstood, and, consequently, that he had been received and noticed as he was."[4] Darcy does not reveal the truth of Wickham's dark nature, so everyone believes him upright, honorable, and trustworthy. Consequently Darcy feels responsible for what happens with Lydia. He discreetly takes measures to expend the finances necessary for Wickham to marry Lydia and expects nothing in return. This is the essence of selfless love.

Even though Darcy anticipates no recompense, the respect, admiration, and growing love that he gains from Elizabeth is worth more than 80 grand or 80 million. Interestingly enough, Elizabeth's expression of thankfulness is what catapults Darcy into renewing his proposal. He assures Elizabeth that he thought only of her when providing for Lydia and that he never intended for her to know what he'd done. So even though Darcy expects nothing, he gains everything. And that's the way "love always protects" works.

Before I know it, my kids will be 16 and 18. They'll be young adults driving themselves around and choosing what colleges they'll attend. And I'll once again look back and be thankful. While the choices I am making limit my career, true love means a relinquishment of the self. The intimate relationship I have with my kids is worth everything and more. Like Darcy, I'll have no regrets and will remain so consumed by love I won't miss what I've sacrificed.

> *Money is not required to buy one necessity of the soul.*
> ~ HENRY DAVID THOREAU ~

---

1. Debra White Smith, *First Impressions* (Eugene, OR: Harvest House, 2004), pp. 284-85.

2. Jane Austen, *Pride and Prejudice*, The Complete Novels of Jane Austen, vol. I (New York: The Modern Library, 1992), pp. 504-05.

3. Ibid., p. 503.

4. Ibid., p. 503.

Love always trusts…

Edmund Bertram and the Friend of a Lifetime

You may be deceived if you trust too much, but you will live in torment if you don't trust enough.
~ FRANK CRANE ~

My husband, Daniel, and I have known of each other most of our lives. Our parents knew each other before we were born. Daniel's parents were thrilled when our family moved back to east Texas and started attending church at my father's home church, which is where Daniel's family attended. When sparks started flying between Daniel and me, our parents were glad. I was 15 and Daniel was 19. So we go back a long way.

I'll never forget my first date with Daniel. He took me to El Chico's restaurant. This is a well-known Mexican food chain that's predominant in the southern U.S. When we placed our orders, he was so impressed that I not only ordered a large meal, but I ate the whole thing—and that was after enjoying a basket of chips and salsa for an appetizer.

He thought, *Wow! I'm going to like this girl. She eats as much as I do!*

During our dating years I remember going to a pizza parlor and ordering two medium pizzas—mine and his. We both ate most of them. The waitress was impressed, to say the least. Then there was the Chinese restaurant where the waitress nearly had a stroke when we ordered enough for four people. We wound up eating all that too! We were a couple of eating machines. Looking back, I don't know how I managed to stay trim and Daniel kept his athlete's physique, but somehow we did.

Unfortunately, our portions have had to get smaller as we get older, and both our sizes have altered a bit...but not too much. We would both love to be eating machines our whole lives.

These and many other fond memories fill the tapestry of our past. Like Fanny Price and Edmund Bertram in *Mansfield Park*, our relationship goes back to much younger days. Interestingly enough, Edmund and Fanny started out as friends, and that friendship grew into a romance. Daniel and I started out with a romance that grew into a deep and lasting friendship that transcends any I have ever known. William Penn said it well: "She is but half a wife that is not, nor is capable of being, a friend." That truth holds for husbands as well. I'm sure Fanny Price would agree:

> *Fanny's friendship was all that [Edmund] had to cling to...Scarcely had he done regretting Mary Crawford, and observing to Fanny how impossible it was that he should ever meet with such another woman, before it began to strike him*

whether a very different kind of woman might not do just as well, or a great deal better; whether Fanny herself were not growing as dear, as important to him in all her smiles and all her ways, as Mary Crawford had ever been; and whether it might not be possible, a hopeful undertaking to persuade her that her warm and sisterly regard for him would be foundation enough for wedded love...Edmund did cease to care about Miss Crawford, and became as anxious to marry Fanny as Fanny herself could desire...

Even in the midst of his late infatuation, he had acknowledged Fanny's mental superiority What must be his sense of it now, therefore! She was of course only too good for him; but as nobody minds having what is too good for them, he was very steadily earnest in the pursuit of the blessing.[1]

When a husband and wife are friends, they enjoy being together, supporting each other, and trusting each other. Any time a married couple searches elsewhere for best friends that offer support and encouragement, that usually indicates the marriage is lacking something important. I'm not saying married people shouldn't have other friends...even great friends. I have numerous friends, both male and female. However, my top pick for the person I most like to hang out with and do things with is my husband because he's my absolute best friend.

A major part of a solid marriage also involves trust. Just as my husband and I have grown into a trust through the years, so Fanny and Edmund grow in their trust of each other. What is so interesting in *Mansfield Park* is to watch Edmund exhibit a complete and unwavering trust of Fanny that he seems oblivious to. As the plot unfolds, the reader clearly sees that Edmund puts more faith in Fanny and her opinions than in any other person in his life. This faith plays out in a model that classically exhibits some strong elements of trust, including trusting her wisdom, her loyalty, and her virtue.

> *Woe to the man whose heart has not learned while young to hope, to love—and to put its trust in life.*
> ~ Joseph Conrad ~

Elements of Trust

Trusting Your Partner's Wisdom

One of the things my husband and I have grown into is consulting each other about nearly everything. Most of the time we each do what the other one thinks is wisest. More often than not, the asker is already thinking in the direction the spouse indicates and the spouse's wisdom confirms what direction is needed.

Since I have an online bookstore, I often carry titles besides my own. The other day, I had an opportunity to purchase a classic, 4-in-1 collection of self-help books that have transformed my life and the lives of millions. I was invited to purchase these books at a fraction of the cost and was tempted to buy all the distributor had—more than 500 books. Before I did so, I consulted my husband. Daniel didn't think I should buy that many copies. However, I really thought I should because I could give them away for ministry and also as a part of my bookstore deals. When I expressed to him how I really thought I should go ahead and buy the books, he laughed and said, "Then why are you asking me?"

I laughed, too, and said, "Yeah, that's pretty good isn't it? I ask your opinion and then argue with you."

We weren't in a heated argument, just two married folks looking at all sides of the issue. In the end, I bought all the distributor had. That was one time when I didn't go with what Daniel said. And there have been a few times he's done the same as well.

In a healthy marriage or relationship, each partner trusts the wisdom of the other and respects the other enough to ask his or her opinion. But each partner also has the freedom to do what he (or she) believes is best in his area of expertise. The majority of the time, my husband and I usually do what the other thinks. But when that doesn't happen, we both give each other the freedom to disagree and to make the decision he or I believes is best.

Fanny and Edmund exhibit the exact same strategy long before they ever commit to marriage. I'm dubbing them the couple who exhibits the "Model Marriage."

When Edmund's brother, Tom, and Mr. Yates, the Bertram sisters, and the Crawfords all decide to put on a play titled *Lover's Vows*, they pressure Edmund into taking a part in the play. Because he objects to the immoral elements in the play, Edmund refuses to participate and will not support even the idea of the play. Fanny is in full agreement.

However, when Tom decides to pull in another member of the community, Charles Maddox, to play opposite Mary Crawford, Edmund crumbles. Thoughts of exposing a person from the community—a stranger—to the risqué nature of the play, makes him blush with shame. Furthermore, the male–female part will require an intimacy between Mary Crawford and Charles Maddox that Mary will find highly uncomfortable. Truth be known, so will Edmund. After he agrees to play the part opposite Mary, his sisters view his decision as jealousy driven.

But before he makes his decision known, he consults Fanny and asks for her wisdom in the matter. The two have built a long-term trust of each other's wisdom, which is manifested in their conversation and the aftermath of it. When Edmund arrives in The East Room to speak with Fanny, she remains against the whole idea and tells him, "I am sorry for Miss Crawford; but I am more sorry to see you drawn in to do what you had resolved against, and what you are known to think will be disagreeable to my uncle. It will be such a triumph to the others!"[2]

Edmund does get Fanny to agree that his taking the part will bring about the good of limiting the play's knowledge to just their group and stopping the countryside from learning about the risqué acting. However, he cannot get her to agree that his taking the part is a good idea. In the face of her continual hesitation he says, "Give me your approbation, then, Fanny. I am not comfortable without it…If you are against me, I ought to distrust myself…"[3] Then he goes on once again to defend his choice by highlighting the embarrassment Miss Crawford will be saved.

Like me and the book purchase, Edmund decides to do what he wants to do anyway. Purchasing books isn't nearly as big a deal as participating in a sexually suggestive play. Therefore, Edmund doesn't fare so well. When he leaves, Fanny decides that

> he had told her the most extraordinary, the most inconceivable, the most unwelcome news; and she could think of nothing else. To be acting! After all his objections—objections so just and so public! After all that she had heard him say, and seen him look, and known him to be feeling. Could it be possible? Edmund so inconsistent! Was he not deceiving himself? Was he not wrong? Alas! it was all Miss Crawford's doing.[4]

In so many words, Fanny thinks Edmund has gone nuts. And she attributes it all to his growing attraction to Miss Crawford and her influence on him. When Edmund's father arrives home from the Indies and discovers the folly of his offspring and their pals, Edmund realizes he should have listened to Fanny's wisdom.

The crucial lines in the whole ordeal are those where Edmund indicates that he cannot be at peace in his decision without consulting Fanny and receiving her blessing. Edmund trusts Fanny's opinion and her wisdom. Even when he is distracted by Mary Crawford to the point of being daft, Edmund manifests the foundation for his lasting love and fulfilling marriage with Fanny. He just doesn't wake up to that love for 120 pages.

Trusting Your Partner's Virtue

My husband has a home-based locksmith business that gets him into the community quite a bit. This business gives him the freedom to set his own hours so he can also manage our ministry and travel. It's also an outlet for his mechanical-oriented gifts. He's a guy who enjoys doing stuff with his hands and will probably always have some sort of side endeavor to release this gift.

Because of the nature of this business, he is frequently asked to change locks for people. Often the lock changing involves a situation where a man or woman is ending a relationship with a person who has a key to his or her house. Therefore, when the locks are changed, the former significant other is unable to enter the premises.

One time a man called him to change the locks on his house. When Daniel arrived, the man explained that he had just discovered that his wife, Pam, was having an affair. Jeff found out because the wife of the man Pam was having an affair with, Gail, called him. Gail explained that her husband, Darren, had been having an affair with Pam.

Jeff's immediate response was, "Not my wife. It can't be my wife. My wife would *never* do anything like that." However, Gail had enough proof to convince Jeff that his wife was indeed having an affair.

So Jeff and Gail decided to re-key the locks on their houses so their spouses couldn't get in. That's where Daniel came onto the scene. After re-keying the locks, Daniel came home and told me the whole story.

He said, "I never cease to be amazed at the number of people who call me whose marriages are breaking up. It just blows my mind."

In healthy relationships both partners go out of their way to keep their virtue intact. Through the years a few women have made passes at Daniel, and the results are somewhat humorous. He's so uncomfortable he nearly breaks his neck to get away. The last thing he wants to do is even talk to a woman who's on the make.

I feel the same way about men on the prowl. I've learned to distance myself from anyone I believe might be thinking the wrong thing. My rule is to abruptly end any conversation that I sense might be leading to an inappropriate proposition or remark.

Daniel and I are both loyal to each other and have no desire to do anything to compromise that loyalty or give the other a reason to question our virtue. Through the years this has bred a very deep trust in our marriage. I'm sure you strive for this in your relationships, too. Edmund has that same level of trust in Fanny's virtue.

When Edmund's father comes home and discovers that the young people have been rehearsing a risqué play and spending money for props, he becomes exasperated. The next morning Edmund approaches his father to explain everything…including his participation in the play. William Penn noted, "A good End cannot sanctifie evil Means; nor must we ever do Evil, that Good may come of it." Jolted by his father's return, Edmund finally recognizes his error. He realizes he has compromised his better judgment and rationalized his wrong choice by believing good could come out of it.

By this point Fanny has proven to Edmund that he can always trust her virtue and her moral stance for what is right.

She alone stood in the face of her seven contemporaries who participated in the play. On top of that, Aunt Norris, that questionable "saint," joined the pressure and called Fanny ungrateful for not taking a part. Fanny refused to compromise her standards or do what her uncle would deem inappropriate. The very fact that Edmund has such undying trust in Fanny's virtue is the foundation for his trust in her wisdom.

Even though Edmund graciously doesn't criticize the others involved, he venerates Fanny: "We have all been more or less to blame," said he, "every one of us, excepting Fanny. Fanny is the only one who has judged rightly throughout; who has been consistent. *Her* feelings have been steadily against it from first to last. She never ceased to think of what was due to you. You will find Fanny everything you could wish."[5]

At the novel's end, when Edmund realizes how morally bankrupt Mary Crawford is, he comes to see that he cannot trust her opinions because they are based upon marred virtue. In the face of the recently married Maria running off with Henry, Mary's main concern is they aren't more discreet. She's not worried about the sins committed or the people who are hurt; she's more concerned with the look of things.

At that point Edmund knows he has been fooled. He understands that the same trust he has put in Fanny can never be placed in Mary. The contrast between Mary's pseudo-virtue and Fanny's genuine virtue is so clear that Edmund finally realizes he should marry the woman whose virtue he has always trusted—and that woman is Fanny Price.

Trusting Your Partner's Loyalty

With such a regard for her, indeed, as his had long been, a regard founded on the most endearing claims of innocence and helplessness, and completed by every recommendation of growing worth, what could be more natural than the change? Loving, guiding, protecting her, as he had been doing ever since her being ten years old, her mind in so great a degree formed by his care, and her comfort depending on his kindness, an object to him of such close and peculiar interest, dearer by all his own importance with her than anyone else at Mansfield, what was there now to add, but that he should learn to prefer soft, light eyes to sparkling, dark ones. And being always with her, and always talking confidentially, and his feelings exactly in that favourable state which a recent disappointment gives, those soft light eyes could not be very long in obtaining the pre-eminence.[6]

Kin Hubbard states, "Of all the home remedies, a wife is the best." How true that is with Edmund in the aftermath of losing Mary Crawford. He goes home to Fanny, licks his wounds, and finds in her the confidante, friend, and comforter she has always been. In some respects, Fanny is like a wife to Edmund for many years. She is his main supporter and chief cheerer in all that he does. Once Edmund awakens to just how much he depends upon Fanny's loyalty and respect, he realizes he has nurtured her from the time she was ten. And from that time forth, Fanny's constancy has never wavered.

Interestingly enough, Edmund's loyalty to Fanny is just as strong as hers to him. When she needs a horse, he provides it. When she needs a defender from her aunts neglecting her best interest, he is there. When she needs validation to her uncle, Edmund doesn't hesitate. They are there for each other any time the need arises. And that's what healthy relationships are made of.

Often when we think of loyalty in regard to relationships, we think of sexual monogamy. However, loyalty transcends the bedroom and penetrates every fiber of a marriage. Couples who are completely loyal to each other manifest reciprocal emotional support as well as verbal support. When we are verbally loyal to our mates, we don't tear them down to others or discuss their shortcomings with a third party. Instead, we cheer them on and provide a safe haven of home and marriage.

For me, that means I don't discuss my man with my girl-friends. I don't number his faults with others. And I don't criticize or belittle him. If there's an area in our marriage he can improve upon, I approach the discussion with kindness and goodness and bathe it in love. He does the same. The results are a unity and harmony that transcends words...and a trust that transcends time.

---

1. Jane Austen, *Mansfield Park*, The Complete Novels of Jane Austen, vol. I (New York: The Modern Library, 1992), pp. 888, 895-96.

2. Ibid., p. 666.

3. Ibid., p. 667.

4. Ibid., p. 668.

5. Ibid., p. 689.

6. Ibid., pp. 895-96.

Love always hopes...

Marianne Dashwood
and Elvis

In all things it is better to hope than to despair.
~ Johann Wolfgang von Goethe ~

If ever there was a book filled with a bunch of hopers it's *Sense and Sensibility*. Marianne Dashwood hopes Willoughby is in love with her. Colonel Brandon hopes Marianne is in love with him. Willoughby hopes Mrs. Smith will not disinherit him. Elinor Dashwood hopes Edward Ferrars loves her. Lucy Steele hopes to marry someone rich. Edward hopes Lucy *will* marry someone rich—anyone but him. Mrs. Ferrars hopes Edward will marry anyone but Elinor—as long as that "anyone" isn't Lucy Steele. And in the end, Willoughby hopes Marianne can forgive him for breaking her heart.

I'm reminded of my first-grade experience. Brian hoped I was in love with him. I recall slurping my Jello-O straight from my lunch tray and Brian's trembling fingers pulling my hair away from my face. He had such a huge crush on me. But I didn't "crush" him back. That's the way those things go.

I adored Bruce. I'll never forget Bruce. He looked like Elvis. I loved Elvis. My dad was the biggest Elvis fanatic in the world. He collected all of Elvis' original songs on the old 45 records and still has them today. I grew up listening to those 45s and can sing many Elvis songs word for word even now.

Bruce fit right in with my "Elvis appreciation" life experience. He had dark hair and full lips just like Elvis. He was darker complected than Elvis, and his eyes were bright blue, but I forgave him for those discrepancies.

I remember one day I was blessed to sit by Bruce. The whole class was reading aloud at our own paces, which I'm sure got really confusing for some. But not for Bruce and me. Somehow we got in sync and started reading the same text together. We both stopped and smiled at each other. I don't know about Bruce, but that was a romantic moment for me—and just about as romantic as it ever got. If he ever did have a crush on me, I never knew it.

Second grade parted us…and I only saw Bruce once after that.

However, I did continue to sing Elvis songs and have told my dad that my inheritance won't be complete without those old 45s. I think one of my top five favorites is "Teddy Bear."

While Marianne Dashwood is more mature than a first grader, her unrestrained love and guileless hoping are very much that of an innocent adolescent only a few steps removed from childhood. I can imagine her singing a song like "Teddy Bear" to Willoughby and asking him to put a chain around her neck and lead her anywhere. And really, that's very close to what happens.

Due to Marianne's naiveté, she is destined to learn some hard lessons. Unfortunately her hope is of the tragic variety. She winds up placing it in the wrong man and reaps a broken heart (that nearly breaks our hearts). Marianne is a reckless innocent who never imagines that Willoughby doesn't return her love. Her hope is so pure, her love so sure, that she places all her faith in one who is not worthy of that faith. Her artless letter to him when she and Elinor arrive in London alone proves that Marianne's hope is pure:

> *Berkelye Street, January.*
>
> *How surprised you will be, Willoughby, on receiving this! and I think you will feel something more than surprise when you know I am in town. An opportunity of coming hither, though with Mrs. Jennings, was a temptation we could not resist. I wish you may receive this in time to come here to-night, but I will not depend on it. At any rate I shall expect you to-morrow. For the present, adieu. M.D.*[1]

By Marianne's own admission, Willoughby never tells her he loves her or proposes. Nevertheless, she believes in his regard to the point of a familiarity that flies in the face of courting etiquette during Austen's time.

Despite the fact that her relationship with Willoughby fails, out of the whole cast of *Sense and Sensibility*, I give Marianne Dashwood the "Hope Award." Even though she begins the book as an immature young thing, her purity of hope and faith are endearing. When such faith and hope are manifested by both parties in a relationship, there is beauty, there is love. If only one party of a romance exhibits Marianne's surety, then the death of hope occurs. Even though the death of hope drives Marianne into the arms of mourning, she recovers to experience the resurrection of hope. And with the resurrection comes a new level of maturity that ushers her from the world of the adolescent into that of a young woman.

> *Hope is the parent of faith.*
> ~ CYRUS A. BRENTOL ~

The Death of Hope

After my Elvis/Bruce experience, I didn't become romantically interested in another boy until fifth grade. And the only reason why I did then is because we moved to a new town. My father was a pastor, and he accepted a church assignment between Quitman and Greenbriar, Arkansas. All the girls and boys at my new school were into the girlfriend/boyfriend trend. They wanted to know whom I liked. After attending a baseball game and watching some of my male classmates play ball, I decided I could like Brent.

While he was quite cute with dark, fluffy hair and blue eyes, he wasn't anything compared to Bruce. I couldn't see even one hint of a resemblance between him and Elvis. But I figured he'd do.

So I told my friend Theresa that I liked him. She, in turn, agreed to tell him I liked him and see if he liked me in return. She reported back to me that he said, "She is very pretty." My spirits soared! I just knew Brent and I were going to become an item.

I started fifth grade and enjoyed looking at Brent across the room. I convinced myself that he was looking back. This was nearly as romantic as reading in unison with Bruce. However, as time marched on and Brent didn't say a word to me, I wondered if maybe we weren't an item. Then Valentine's Day came, and I picked out a special Valentine just for him. When I went through my Valentine cards, I couldn't find even a scrap of one from him.

My hope wavered. I became a bit suspicious of Brent's commitment to our relationship. A few days later, I decided to send another messenger to see what the deal was. I can't remember who that messenger was, but I recall her going up to him with the key question, "Do you like Debra?"

His response was quite eye-opening. "No! Just like I told Theresa! She's greeny!"

I'd never heard the term "greeny" before, and I haven't heard it since. But it didn't sound like it was any good at all. The expression on his face certainly wasn't.

I realized that Theresa had not been honest with me, probably because she wanted to spare my feelings. But in reality she had built up a hope in me that began a slow death after Valentine's Day and was soon dashed to bits.

When Marianne Dashwood arrives in London she is secure in her love for Willoughby and her hope that they will eventually marry. However, after he doesn't respond to her first letter or appear at the dance to which he is invited and he knows she will be, Marianne finds herself where I was when I didn't get a Valentine from Brent. Her hopes died slowly. Her second letter to him reveals the beginning of that death.

> *I cannot express my disappointment in having missed you the day before yesterday, nor my astonishment at not having received any answer to a note which I sent you above a week ago. I have been expecting to hear from you, and still more to see you, every hour of the day. Pray call again as soon as possible, and explain the reason of my having expected this in vain. You had better come earlier another time, because we are generally out by one. We were last night at Lady Middleton's where there was a dance. I have been told that you were asked to be of the party. But could it be so? You must be very much altered indeed since we parted, if that could be the case, and you not there. But I will not suppose this possible, and I hope very soon to receive your personal assurance of its being otherwise.   M.D.[2]*

According to E.R. Stettinius Jr., "Happiness has many roots, but none more important than security." At this point, Marianne's security in Willoughby's affection is waning. Even though she misses his call, she certainly expects him to attend the dance where he knows she will be...but he doesn't.

Her hope progresses from shaky to being dashed to bits when

she sees Willoughby at the party and he slights her by barely shaking her hand and treating her like a near stranger.

> *"But have you received my notes?" cried Marianne with the wildest anxiety. "Here is some mistake, I am sure—some dreadful mistake. What can be the meaning of it? Tell me, Willoughby—for heaven's sake, tell me, what is the matter?"*

From here, Marianne goes into a tailspin. Then she crashes when she receives Willoughby's reply to her third letter, in which she asks for a definitive answer about their relationship. In essence, Willoughby sends Marianne a "Dear John"…or "Dear Johnna" letter. At this point all the hope Marianne has placed in Willoughby ends. And during the process she states that famous line that few can forget: "Misery such as mine has no pride. I care not who knows that I am wretched. The triumph of seeing me so may be open to all the world…I must feel—I must be wretched."[4]

The loss of a relationship one has banked on as Marianne does, can be as horrible as a death in the family. Once the death of hope happens, the mourning begins. And Marianne Dashwood goes into that season, which merges into an illness that nearly costs her life.

The Resurrection of Hope

Fortunately, I didn't take the loss of Brent too hard. I think I was embarrassed for an hour and disappointed for a day or two. After that I didn't give Brent much thought. Besides, he didn't look like Elvis anyway.

After Brent, there was some boy in the sixth grade (I was still in fifth) who was supposed to be my boyfriend. But all he did was walk with me to the school bus every day. He never said a word to me, and I didn't say a word to him either.

I thought, *This is ridiculous. We aren't talking or anything.* So I relieved him of his silent vigil and broke up with him.

Then there was a short romance with Rob, the guy who never stopped liking me. By seventh grade I talked myself into liking some guy named Harold for a few hours. Then I developed that gargantuan crush on Conner, which lead me to that famous spaghetti scene I mentioned in chapter 1.

The point is that there was still room for the resurrection of hope after the Brent episode. I moved on to other crushes and other interests…until I met Daniel—and he and I ate ourselves right up to the wedding chapel.

The resurrection of Marianne's hope takes a much more mature and direct line—straight to Colonel Brandon. Ironically, the Marianne we meet at the novel's opening has stacks of objections to even considering Brandon as a romantic prospect: He's too old, has had a former romantic attachment, and is far too serious. But the very man whom she objects to is the one whom she places her renewed hopes in.

As she awakens to Brandon's constancy and his love, her fragile hope gradually grows until Marianne agrees to be his wife and, in time, comes to love Brandon as much as she did Willoughby. Brandon's hope and faith in life is restored as well, and he becomes more cheerful and animated. This annuls one of Marianne's original complaints: that he is too serious. As for his having a former romantic attachment, by the novel's end she fits that description herself. Of his being too old, there is nothing Marianne can do about *his* age, but she certainly does her share of maturing, thus making the gap in their ages much less of an issue

Hebrews 11:1 states, "Now faith is being sure of what we hope for and certain of what we do not see." By the end of *Sense and Sensibility*, Austen leaves the distinct impression that Marianne and Brandon both have great hope in their future together. Both of them have had all their hopes dashed, only to be resurrected to new life and new love. Marianne and Brandon both received the fulfillment of their hope, but with a different person than either of them originally chose. This resurrection can occur in our own lives if we allow the Lord to restore what is lost. And when God gives us a vision, we can find daily hope in understanding that He will accomplish what He has shown us in His time and with those whom He chooses.

> *He has made everything beautiful in its time.*
> ~ Ecclesiastes 3:11 ~

---

1. Jane Austen, *Sense and Sensibility*, The Complete Novels of Jane Austen, vol. I (New York: The Modern Library, 1992), p. 131.
2. Ibid., pp. 131-32.
3. Ibid., p. 124.
4. Ibid., p. 133.

Love always perseveres and never fails…

~14~

Mr. Elliot and the Greatest Lovers

And now these three remain: faith, hope and love.
But the greatest of these is love.
~ 1 Corinthians 13:13 ~

I would love to tell you that everything went perfectly smooth in my romance with Daniel. But somewhere between the stacks of pizzas and piles of Mexican food, I wound up breaking Daniel's heart. Like many young, fickle teenagers, I didn't know my own mind and couldn't decide if Daniel really was Mr. Right or not. However, he was four years older, more mature, and very certain that I was Miss Right. At the ripe old age of 17, I broke up with him. Looking back, I can almost hear our families' collective gasps.

Poor Daniel howled at the moon, and somebody should have just slapped some sense into me. Even today, after 23 years of marriage, I've yet to meet a man who measures up to him. Many times other women are in awe of his supportive and considerate ways. What was I thinking way back when? My only excuse was that I was so young, Daniel was really ready to get married, and I just wasn't sure I was ready for that commitment.

Anyway, we got back together and were married when we were the ancient ages of 19 and 23. At the time I thought I was *so* grown up. But now as a 42-year-old woman, I look back and see that I was still just a baby. Furthermore, I'm already encouraging my kids to wait until their mid or late twenties to get married because I believe they'll be more mature and able to make a more solid decision.

But when the love bug bites, it bites. And I did wind up with a phenomenal man of honor despite my young age at marriage. Granted, we both had so many areas we needed growth in, and we gave each other plenty of grief the first decade of our marriage. Neither one of us has ever had an affair, but we have had our share of issues. Nevertheless, after more than two decades of marriage, we're now having the time of our lives! But too often that isn't the case for couples these days.

In Austen's *Persuasion*, when Anne Elliot falls in love with Wentworth and he proposes, her family believes that it won't be the case with them either. Lady Russell talks Anne out of marrying Wentworth because he doesn't have a sizable income, has no fortune, and just isn't good enough for her. So for the sake of family loyalty and doing what is financially prudent, Anne turns down the man of her dreams.

As Jane Austen's tale unfolds, readers fall in love with both

Anne and Wentworth and their poignant story. There's nothing more beautiful than estranged lovers who somehow find each other after years of separated misery. Their love most often grows stronger as the years unfold while their wretchedness without each other achingly increases. Anne Elliot and Captain Wentworth fit this scenario better than any of Austen's other heroes and heroines. I give Anne and Wentworth the "Greatest Lovers Award."

From their first meeting after years of being apart, their latent longing is so strong it's almost tangible. Jane Austen expertly builds and builds and builds their chemistry until we teeter on the edge of our seats. Finally Anne awakens to the realization that Captain Wentworth is jealous of her and her cousin, Mr. Elliot, even though Anne has no desire to marry her cousin.

[Anne and Captain Wentworth] talked for a few minutes more…he even looked down towards the bench, as if he saw a place on it well worth occupying; when at that moment a touch on her shoulder obliged Anne to turn round. It came from Mr. Elliot. He begged her pardon, but she must be applied to, to explain Italian again. Miss Carteret was very anxious to have a general idea of what was next to be sung. Anne could not refuse; but never had she sacrificed to politeness with a more suffering spirit.

A few minutes, though as few as possible, were inevitably consumed; and when her own mistress again, when able to turn and look as she had done before, she found herself accosted by Captain Wentworth, in a reserved yet hurried sort of farewell.

He must wish her good night; he was going; he should get home as fast as he could.

"Is not this song worth staying for?" said Anne, suddenly struck by an idea which made her yet more anxious to be encouraging.

"No!" he replied, impressively, "there is nothing worth my staying for;" and he was gone directly.

Jealousy of Mr. Elliot! It was the only intelligible motive. Captain Wentworth jealous of her affection! Could she have believed it a week ago; three hours ago! For a moment the gratification was exquisite. But alas! there were very different thoughts to succeed. How was such jealousy to be quieted? How was the truth to reach him? How, in all the peculiar disadvantages of their respective situations, would he ever learn her real sentiments? It was misery to think of Mr. Elliot's attentions. Their evil was incalculable.[1]

By this point the romance between these two has persevered through years of separation and Captain Wentworth's almost being trapped into a guilt-driven engagement to Louisa Musgrove, a rash young lady who flirts with Wentworth and then jumps to her near death. When Wentworth can't catch her, he blames himself. Anne watches in misery as she observes Wentworth's feelings of obligation. Then she goes back to the city of Bath, certain that she's finally lost him to the arms of another.

Just as Anne fears that Wentworth will marry Louisa, so Wentworth fears that Anne will marry Mr. Elliot. But Louisa finally marries someone else, and Wentworth follows Anne to Bath. From there the sparks fly. When Anne recognizes

Wentworth's jealousy, she realizes his love and strains for any means to bridge their past relationship into the present and regain what the years have taken. According to Thornton Wilder, "There is a land of the living and a land of the dead and the bridge is love, the only survival, the only meaning."

Amazingly, Anne and Wentworth's love survives all obstacles, including time. The two of them persist until their hearts become one, and together they fully embrace the land of the living. Their love never fails; it perseveres against all odds until the two are united. The qualities of their perseverance are what earn them the "Greatest Lovers Award." They pursue their original goal, don't bow to obstacles, and ultimately overcome discouragement.

> *I hold it true whate'er befall;*
> *I feel it, when I sorrow most;*
> *'Tis better to have loved and lost*
> *Than never to have loved at all.*
> ~ Alfred, Lord Tennyson ~

They Pursue Their Original Goal

Among his other attributes, my husband is very much mechanically inclined. Daniel can fix almost anything. If he's never fixed it before, most of the time he can tear it apart and figure out how to fix it. I have hero-worship respect for his abilities.

Through the years there have only been a few things that broke around our house that he wasn't able to fix. I was as aghast as Superman fans would be if Superman looked at the crowd and said, "I can't fly that high." But apparently Daniel's skills are limited when it comes to fixing central air units and some thingy on the clothes dryer he didn't know about. Other than that, the guy has *the gift!*

I'm reminded of a series of *The Cosby Show* episodes when Vanessa decides she's going to marry a guy named Dabnis. Vanessa has just gone away to college, and she's only 18 when she comes home to tell her family that she's engaged. At first her family is shocked and against the whole thing.

But after they meet Dabnis, their opinions gradually change. See, Dabnis is as big of a handyman as Daniel. The guy can fix anything. Soon Cliff Huxstable has him working on all sorts of problems around the house. Cliff's wife, Clair, grows enamored with Dabnis, and so do Cliff's parents. Dabnis is the man of the hour…the fix-anything hero.

The whole lot of them start celebrating Vanessa's marriage to Dabnis and can't wait until the wedding. They even start brainstorming about when the wedding should happen! At this point Vanessa feels uncomfortably pressured to marry Dabnis, even though she's the one who agreed to the engagement. The wedding scenario loses its forbidden appeal in the light of her whole family shoving her down the aisle. The engagement is broken.

Unfortunately, Anne Elliot's family doesn't feel this way about Frederick Wentworth. "The way to love anything is to realize it might be lost," says Gilbert K. Chesterton. Anne and Wentworth not only realize their love might be lost, it *is* lost. Well, their marriage is lost anyway. Their love continues to thrive beneath layers of "what if's" and "I wish I had's" that the years produce.

In the end their love is rekindled with a fierce and undying passion, and Wentworth and Anne awaken to their original intent to love, honor, and cherish until death do they part. From this point on, neither of them shrinks from the pursuit of this goal. After Wentworth is freed of obligations related to Louisa's near-tragic jump, he goes after his woman.

The minute Anne sees him, a sweet yearning springs upon her, and she nearly can't believe her eyes. "Still, however, she had enough to feel! It was agitation, pain, pleasure; something between delight and misery."[2] When Wentworth speaks to her, she doesn't shrink away, which is more in line with her personality. Even in the face of awkward embarrassment, she returns his greeting and has a brief conversation.

Later, when they both arrive at the same concert, Wentworth openly talks to Anne. They converse about Louisa, and he doesn't shy from hinting that he never cared for her romantically. After their conversation is broken up by Lady Dalrymple's entrance and they part, Anne later actively looks for Wentworth but doesn't find him. She consoles herself with the assurance that *he will* find her before the evening is over.

When he does, their conversation is interrupted by Mr. Elliot. Wentworth gets jealous, and when he tries to hurriedly depart, Anne doesn't allow him to walk off without a plea that holds the undertones of "Please stay": "'Is not this song worth staying for?' said Anne, suddenly struck by an idea which made her more anxious to be encouraging."[3] In very subtle yet obvious steps toward each other, Wentworth and Anne begin to pursue their original goal...that their hearts be united as one.

One of the things I've learned in life is that people don't get anything accomplished unless they keep their original goal in focus. Too many times when I've set a goal or I believe God has shown me a goal, there are all sorts of happenings that can distract me from my plans. Anne and Wentworth are a wonderful example of a couple who has their original goal derailed. However, they eventually do get back on track and pursue each other. One thing we learn from them is that we can always adjust our path, refocus, and once again move toward the original goal.

All too often people throw their hands into the air and quit after their paths have been altered. But, as one of my pastors once said, "God always honors the direction you're going." Therefore, I believe His blessings are upon us when we regroup, recommit, and begin again to try to reach our goals. Remember, the only person who can fuel your quitting is you. Quitting is what failure is made of. Perseverance is what makes people achieve their dreams.

They Don't Bow to Obstacles

After I broke up with Daniel, we both started dating other people. I really don't think Daniel *wanted* to date anyone else but he did because I did. I remember him telling me that he went to Six Flags Over Texas on a church trip with another girl. He realized part of the way through the day that he kept saying stuff like "Debra and I have ridden that ride." I'm sure that really blessed his date.

During that season we did still see each other. When we were together, Daniel always made it vividly clear that he wanted us to go steady again. He kept pursuing me despite my fickleness. He didn't bow to the obstacles I placed in our relationship. Instead he kept his focus on the prize—me! His pursuit paid off. Now, 23 years of marriage later, he's still stuck with me.

Anne and Wentworth also have some serious obstacles to their courtship and marriage. Like I broke my Daniel's heart, Anne breaks Wentworth's. But her motives involve Lady Russell and her father's disapproval.

At this point in her life, Anne is too young and too impressionable to stand up to her aunt and father. She allows the obstacles to end her and Wentworth's romance, with Wentworth kicking and screaming in protest. In the face of Frederick Wentworth's pain at the breakup, "[Anne] had to encounter all the additional pain of opinions, on his side, totally unconvinced and unbending, and of his feeling himself ill-used by so forced a relinquishment."[4]

However, when they come together again after years of separation, both are more mature and more in love than ever. Douglas Jerrold said it best: "Love's like the measles, all the worse when it comes late." For Anne and Wentworth, it comes early but hits even harder the second time around.

And in the throes of the relapse, they face the obstacles and refuse to bow to them. Wentworth is no idiot. He well understands that Anne's family still thinks him beneath her. Elizabeth, Anne's older, snobby sister, spends most of the book snubbing him. Only at the book's end does she extend an invitation to him. And by then she realizes he's grown into a man of fortune, name, and consequence. However, Wentworth is not impressed. His expression toward her is one of contempt. I'm sure he's thinking, "If you can't value me when you think I'm a nobody, then you don't value me at all." Wentworth is not falling all over himself to cater to and please Anne's family. He faces them and Lady Russell and, this time, doesn't let them get in the way.

As for Anne, she fully knows that Lady Russell still disapproves of the match with Wentworth and thinks she should marry Mr. Elliot, become Lady Elliot, inherit Kellynch Hall and all the privileges that go with the whole package. Lady Russell has forgone subtle hints about Anne marrying her cousin and is quite outspoken. The 19-year-old Anne very likely would have quietly and meekly carried out Lady Russell's wishes, but Anne is no longer 19. She knows her own mind and her own heart. With calm assurance, Anne ignores Lady Russell's advice, declines the prospect of marrying Mr. Elliot, and accepts Wentworth.

Have you overcome obstacles in your search for love and contentment? I've known people who, when faced with obstacles, interpret them as a divine sign that they must stop pursuing their goal. In reality, any time we identify goals in our lives there will be significant obstacles. Most worthy goals are not achieved without the necessity of overcoming obstacles. While it is important to understand that divine guidance can sometimes come in the form of obstacles erected to end a pursuit, the wise person entertains various reasons for the holdup.

The best and most error-proof way to determine if an obstacle should be heeded is time. Rushing headlong into any situation while navigating obstacles isn't normally prudent—unless there's a tornado on your tail and you're running to the storm cellar. However, a season of waiting before the Father and reflecting upon motives and outcome usually proves whether or not an obstacle should be circumvented or heeded. When we firmly believe God has inspired the goal in the first place, the obstacles should not be bowed to but rather should be overcome.

Time was the test for Anne and Wentworth. While a few weeks or months often supplies sufficient time for us to determine the nature of the obstacles, they waited almost a decade. When they did overcome the impediments, they'd never been surer of their love. Wentworth offers himself to Anne again "with a heart even more your own than when you almost broke it, eight years and a half ago."[5]

They Overcome Discouragement

Who can be in doubt of what followed? When any two young people take it into their heads to marry, they are pretty sure by perseverance to carry their point, be they ever so poor, or ever so imprudent, or ever so little likely to be necessary to each other's ultimate comfort…How should a Captain Wentworth and an Anne Elliot, with the advantage of maturity of mind, consciousness of right, and one independent fortune between them, fail of bearing down every opposition?"[6]

Indeed, Anne and Captain Wentworth do persevere and bear down every discouragement. What could be more disheartening than having the love of your life ripped away from you, and forever after using that person as a measuring stick for every other romantic prospect that is met? By Wentworth's own admission, he never believes he's seen Anne's equal, let alone anyone better than she or more suited to him.

Even though Anne isn't broadly exposed to other bachelors and matrimonial prospects, she spends years believing she should have accepted Wentworth's proposal. Anne realizes the loss of her love. And that loss is magnified when Wentworth appears back in her life and seems to be forming an attachment with Louisa. Anne's discouragement increases when Louisa incurs a head injury and Wentworth blames himself. By Anne's own assumption and everyone else's, Wentworth appears on the brink of proposing to Louisa.

Yet Louisa falls for another, and Wentworth is once again free to pursue his lady. Finally, after Wentworth's facing his jealousy of Mr. Elliot and Anne's facing continued pressure from Lady Russell to marry Mr. Elliot, Wentworth overcomes all and states his heart in a letter—but only after Anne's own words encourage him to make the move. And his letter sparks the reconciliation and renewed avowal of love that is eight-and-a-half years coming.

I can listen no longer in silence. I must speak to you by such means as are within my reach. You pierce my soul. I am half agony, half hope. Tell me not that I am too late, that such precious feelings are gone for ever. I offer myself to you again with a heart even more your own than when you almost broke it, eight years and half ago. Dare not say that man forgets sooner than woman, that his love has an earlier death. I have loved none but you... Too good, too excellent creature! You do us justice, indeed. You do believe that there is true attachment and constancy among men. Believe it to be most fervent, most undeviating...[7]

If Wentworth had never written the letter the two of them could have floated along for weeks without a reconciliation. But he takes a chance. He overcomes discouragement and doubts and makes his move. The end result is that his love doesn't fail. Wentworth has persevered to the end, and he wins the love of his life.

Too many times the battle is fought and lost in the mind. Our own discouragement makes us doubt that we can overcome obstacles. We lose sight of our goal. It's much safer not to take the chance...not to step out of our comfort zones. But I've found that most everything worth having involves deliberately facing the awkwardness through faith.

A friend once told me, "Debra, when you have a problem, you grab it by the horns and throw it to the ground." I laughed. But the truth is, if you don't grab your problems and deal with them, *they'll* grab *you* and try to take you down.

> *A coward is incapable of exhibiting love;*
> *it is the prorogative of the brave.*
>
> ~ Mahatma Gandhi ~

1. Jane Austen, *Persuasion*, The Complete Novels of Jane Austen, vol. II (New York: The Modern Library, 1992), p. 666.

2. Ibid., p. 655.

3. Ibid., p. 666.

4. Ibid., p. 549.

5. Ibid., p. 700.

6. Ibid., p. 708.

7. Ibid., pp. 700-01.

⌐ Dear Jane... ⌐

From what I understand, you spent the day before your death writing. Your brother says, "She wrote whilst she could hold a pen, and with a pencil when a pen was become too laborious. The day preceding her death she composed some stanzas replete with fancy and vigour."[1] I guess you and I have a few things in common. Not the dead part. I'm not dead yet (I know some days that's questionable), but really, I have no intentions of going to Deadville any time soon. What we have in common is that it sounds like you were as much of a writing maniac as I am. I've said for many years that when they put me in the casket, my corpse will probably pop back up in computer posture, with my hands in front of me, my shoulders hunched, my face straining forward, as if I'm pushing for that last sentence.

I think that's because writing gets in your blood and stays there. I'm certainly glad that was the case with you. You had so much to give! You've taught me leagues about rich writing and even a thing or two about love...as well as how to craft 50 or so romance novels.

As much as I love reading your books, I also adore curling up in front of the fireplace on a winter's evening with a bowl of popcorn, some hot cocoa, and a Jane Austen movie. I love the way the movies bring a new dimension to your work and your characters. I always ache for Knightley's unrequited love for Emma…celebrate the sparkling excitement between Darcy and Elizabeth…long for Edmund to wake up to Fanny Price's undying love…and cheer for Elinor Dashwood as she learns to love Edward with abandonment. I sigh when Anne Elliot and Captain Wentworth are finally reunited…and laugh out loud at the forever naive and dear Catherine Morland as she bungles her way into Henry Tilney's heart.

What a cast of characters. What a writer. What a woman you were. I can only languish over the novels you never wrote due to your early departure from this world. But the novels you did write have forever left an impression upon my mind, my heart, and my writing.

One of the patterns I have used over and over again when writing about the attraction between the sexes is based upon that wonderful dance scene when Darcy and Elizabeth have that deliciously witty exchange:

> *He smiled, and assured her that whatever she wished him to say should be said.*
>
> *"Very well. That reply will do for the present. Perhaps by and by I may observe that private balls are much pleasanter than public ones. But now we may be silent."*
>
> *"Do you talk by rule, then, while you are dancing?"*
>
> *"Sometimes. One must speak a little, you know. It would look odd to be entirely silent for half an hour together and yet for*

*the advantage of some, conversation ought to be so arranged, as
that they may have the trouble of saying as little as possible."*

   *"Are you consulting your own feelings in the present case,
or do you imagine that you are gratifying mine?"*

   *"Both," replied Elizabeth, archly; "for I have always seen
a great similarity in the turn of our minds. We are each of an
unsocial, taciturn disposition, unwilling to speak, unless we
expect to say something that will amaze the whole room, and
be handed down to posterity with all the 'éclat of a proverb."*

   *"This is no very striking resemblance of your own character, I
am sure," said he. "How near it may be to mine, I cannot pretend
to say. You think it a faithful portrait undoubtedly."*

   "I must not decide on my own performance." [2]

After this banter, Darcy and Elizabeth are silent until they
come back together. While the tension is high and the attraction is
electric, these two continue to come together and pull apart as they
move in rhythm and sequence to that nineteenth-century dance.

Nearly every time I write a novel that includes romance, I
recall that dance scene and I have my hero and heroine "come
together," then "pull apart." Each time they come together, they're
a bit closer. When they pull apart it's a little less. Then there's
always that scene at the end when they pull so far apart you just
don't know if they can overcome their differences. But finally,
they always do—just like Darcy and Elizabeth.

As you so eloquently put it, "When any two young people
take it into their heads to marry, they are pretty sure by perseverance to carry their point."[3] In other words, love always wins, and
this is certainly true in your novels. The power of love conquers

all and gives us hope that the same can and will happen in our lives. While you demonstrate this with your major characters, even your secondary characters prove to be strong reminders of this truth. Colonel Brandon and Marianne Dashwood overcome their age differences; Jane Bennet and Charles Bingley persevere despite the interference of a well-meaning Darcy; and Robert Martin's patience finally pays off when Harriet Smith decides he's her man despite Emma's opinions.

Thanks, Jane, for all your tremendous characters, their phenomenal stories, and your earnest portrayal of love and romance. Thanks for motivating and teaching and for being that good, literary friend I can always rely on…never changing, but forever enlightening or comforting as the need may arise. In your own immortal words, "When a young lady is to be a heroine, the perverseness of forty surrounding families cannot prevent her. Something must and will happen to throw a hero in her way."[4] Anytime such a fictional young lady pops into my mind, I can always rely on you to provide the inspiration to create both the lady and her hero in a way that wins my own heart…and hopefully the hearts of my readers.

> Your devoted fan,
> *Debra White Smith*

---

1. Foreword, *The Complete Novels of Jane Austen*, vol. I (New York: Random House, 1992), p. vi.
2. Jane Austen, *Pride and Prejudice*, The Complete Novels of Jane Austen, vol. I (New York: Modern Library, 1992), p. 338.
3. Jane Austen, *Persuasion*, The Complete Novels of Jane Austen, vol. II (New York: Modern Library, 1992), p. 708.
4. Jane Austen, *Northanger Abbey*, The Complete Novels of Jane Austen, vol. II (New York: Modern Library, 1992). p. 360.